JUSTIN
TIMBERLAKE
THE UNOFFICIAL BOOK
MARTIN ROACH

First published in Great Britain in 2003 by
Virgin Books Ltd
Thames Wharf Studios
Rainville Road
London
W6 9HA

A catalogue record for this book is available from
the British Library.

ISBN 1 85227 029 2

Designed by Egelnick and Webb
Printed and bound in Great Britain by
The Bath Press, CPI Group

Photographs: Redferns: end papers, 51, 72
(Stuart Mostyn), 16 (Jon Super), 41, 69 (Christina
Radish); LFI: 5, 56 (Dennis Van Tine), 18 (Kevin
Mazur - Umaz), 31(L) (Anthony Dixon), 31(R),
42, 48, 61(R) (Jen Lowery - Ulow), 33 (Ron Wolfson
URW), 34; Retna Ltd. USA: 7, 9(L&R), 28(R)
(Bernhard Kuhmstedt), 38-39 (Lillian Bonomo),
62 (Tammie Arroyo/AFF), 78(L) (Gary Gershoff),
61(L) (Buhe/Vanit), 67; Famous: 11, 52 (Pauline
French); Corbis: 12-13, 15 (S.I.N.), 23 (Pacha),
27 (Ethan Miller), reverse end paper (Steve
Azara/Corbis Sygma); Rex Features: 20(L) (Sipa
Press), 20-21 (Mark Von Holden/DMI), 24-25,
59, 76 (Peter Brooker), 28(L) (S Gaboury/DMI),
45 (John Roca), 47, 48(R) (Charles Knight), 55
(Mirek Towski/DMI), 65, 71, 75 (Richard Young),
79 (Stewart Cook); Star File: 36 (Vincent Zuffante).

CONTENTS

INTRODUCTION

'This past year has been all about change. Big change. I ended a four-year relationship. I bought a house in LA. I embarked on a solo career and, on top of it all, I did it all in front of the world, without losing my head. It's been really good.'

Justin Timberlake, December 2002

Justin Timberlake is a rarity in music: a genuine pop chameleon. He is the front man in the world's biggest boy band but is also fêted by the most cynical of music critics. His lean and sultry image can artfully grace stylish photo shoots in fashion monthlies, yet at the same time he can easily dominate the world's teen mags, which gleefully divulge his favourite colour and the name of his pet dog. Hip-hop gurus and soul and R&B experts dissect his solo album in minute detail while all the time the tabloids automatically relegate almost every other celebrity to the insides of their publications, so that the latest gossip on Justin's complex love life can be plastered across their front pages.

While many stars are proud of their achievements in switching between such audiences from one project to another, Justin Timberlake seems able to perform such career acrobatics from one interview to the next. It is a rare feat indeed. How has Justin, a mummy's boy from Memphis and former children's TV star, morphed himself into the most exciting, acclaimed and diverse superstar of the twenty-first century? It is a strange story indeed . . .

CHAPTER 1:
MEMPHIS SINGS TR

BLUES

'I JUST HATED MY HAIR. PEOPLE USED TO CALL ME BRILLO PAD'

The year 1981 saw the fairy-tale wedding of Prince Charles and Lady Diana Spencer, an assassination attempt on the Pope and the launch of a television channel dedicated to non-stop music videos, called MTV. On the last day of the first month of that year, Justin Randall Timberlake made his entrance into the world, in a small family home in a suburban satellite town just outside Memphis, Tennessee. His mother, Lynn, was only twenty.

He shares his birthday with a most unlikely fellow star – the Sex Pistols' Johnny Rotten (albeit 25 years earlier). His place of birth was auspicious enough for a future pop icon, Memphis being the hometown of Jerry Lee Lewis, Aretha Franklin, Maurice White of Earth, Wind And Fire and, most famously of all, Elvis Presley. The city is a cradle of the blues and soul.

Unfortunately for Justin, his family environment was not so perfect at first. In 1983, when he was just two, his mother, Lynn, and father, Randy Timberlake, got divorced. Two years later, Lynn married a local banker, Paul Harless, and the four-year-old Justin settled down into a very happy new family life. His bond with his mother's new husband has never been weaker for him being his stepdad; he says 'I do speak to my biological father sometimes, but Paul is like my real dad . . . he's always been there for me.' Indeed, having a financial brain in the family proved to be quite an asset by the time Justin was earning prodigious amounts of money as a pop star, but for now Paul provided a steady and welcome stability at home. Justin's real father, Randy, also remarried – a lady named Lisa, who later gave birth to two stepbrothers for Justin: Stephen and Jonathan.

Justin's mother played several instruments, so music was a constant feature in the family home (it was rumoured that her father played bass for The King, but this is not true). The first signs of Justin's future talent came early. Lynn noticed that her young son, at the age of eight, was constantly humming along to the car radio on the way to school. Keen to encourage his apparent creativity, she enrolled him at singing lessons. Justin was already following in his father's footsteps – Randy Timberlake was an accomplished bluegrass singer, an influence that's plain to see in his son's later work.

Justin went to E.E. Jeter Elementary School until the age of twelve. He was a typical young boy; he says, 'I'd turn the light off, and run for my bed. About six feet before I'd get there, I'd

leap as far as I could and get on the bed. I always had this fear of having this gremlin's arm reach out from under the bed and grab my leg.'

Justin's trademark curly locks were actually the cause of much schoolyard mockery during his formative years. Unoriginally nicknamed 'Curly', he was a classic case of an ugly duckling, if ever there was one (other nicknames have included Butter, Bounce and The Baby). Although now, two decades later, he is established as one of the world's most desirable men, at the time his appearance was a real burden, as he told Associated Press: 'I just hated my hair. People used to call me Brillo Pad.' At one point he became so sick of the bullying that he took out some paper scissors and hacked at the curls in frustration, cutting most of them off. To make matters worse, he suffered acne and, when he

wasn't being called 'Brillo Pad', he was being derided as 'Pizza Face'. His only route to acceptance was that he was a great basketball player, a sport that remains his favourite to this day. Nonetheless, 'Curly' was often a quiet child who walked around with his head held down, 'so you never saw anything but the top of his head,' according to his mum.

The epitome of urban cool and modern sex appeal JT may now be, but at the tender age of ten his entire world revolved around one ambition – to win a role on *The Mickey Mouse Club* and thus become a 'Mouseketeer'.

The young, aspiring Justin had been diligently taking his vocal lessons and was obsessed with the idea of becoming a superstar. He'd been busying himself on the tiring and ruthless

RELATIONSHIPS BECAME INTIMATE VERY QUICKLY

children's audition circuit and even enjoyed some small successes such as a 1993 appearance on the talent show *Star Search*, a prototype for *Pop Idol* (unfortunately he lost out to a young girl who sang a Broadway song). He'd also done a brief stint in a New Kids On The Block tribute band, which was an ironic choice of career move in light of his future fame with 'N Sync.

However, it was a role in Disney's *The Mickey Mouse Club* that was his ultimate goal. Any self-respecting young wannabe was desperate to win a part in this irreverent children's show, which mixed comedy sketches with covers of current hits sung by the child stars – an odd combination but one that was a ratings winner nonetheless. *The Mickey Mouse Club* has since proved to be a remarkable breeding ground for future stars. As well as providing the springboard for 'N Sync, the show also discovered Christina Aguilera, Keri Russell of *Felicity* fame and Ryan Gosling from *Young Hercules*. More notably, from JT's perspective, the show also gave his future girlfriend, Britney Spears, her first big break.

When a nine-year-old Britney first attended the nerve-wracking open audition for *MMC*, the queue was two thousand kids long. She made it through to the final six but was then told she

would not be offered a job. When she returned for another audition a year later, unbeknown to her, another aspiring hopeful was behind her in the snaking queue: one Justin Timberlake.

So eager was Justin to win the part that he and his mother had temporarily moved to Orlando to pursue the dream. On that fateful audition day, when he finally got to the front of the lengthy queue, he belted out a rousing version of 'When a Man Loves a Woman'. His performance was superb and much to his, and his mother's, delight, he was offered a role in season six of *MMC*, which meant beginning work immediately. At the time, the show was presented by Washington DC-born Joshua Scott Chasez, known as JC, who won the role aged only thirteen and was the lead for four years.

The prize of being a Mouseketeer did not come without demands for the excitable recruits, which necessarily thrust these very young wannabes into an overtly adult environment. A typical working week would involve five days' hard graft, starting with the 7 a.m. bus to the studio's own school on the lot, then three hours' study before rehearsals all afternoon, with make-up and wardrobe sessions preparing them for the actual show itself. This was filmed in front

of a live audience over a further three hours at Disney's MGM Studios. Once that was wrapped up, despite having been awake since 6 a.m., the kids would return to their parents with a homework schedule to complete, before starting all over again the next morning. In this intense environment, relationships became intimate very quickly and, though it might seem unlikely with the benefit of hindsight, Britney Spears and Christina Aguilera developed a close bond. More pertinent to the Timberlake story, however, so too did he and Ms Spears.

The Mickey Mouse Club was abruptly cancelled in 1995, despite still enjoying strong ratings. When interviewed later about the effect of this bitter disappointment on the cast of young hopefuls, Christina Aguilera showed a rare degree of foresight. 'We used to joke around backstage and say, "Whenever the show ends, we'll all go off our separate ways and become stars."' And that's exactly what they did do.

Very young stars have often found life after fame difficult to handle, for obvious reasons. Gary Coleman from *Diff'rent Strokes* and Drew Barrymore are just two examples of pre-teen and teen stars whose lives were turned upside down after the spotlight of their prodigious careers moved on. After *The Mickey Mouse Club* was cancelled, Justin was hardly a destitute, broken ego, but he did admit to becoming depressed when the demanding but exciting whirlwind that had dominated his life finished. 'One day I broke down. I was crying and crying and I didn't know why. Luckily, my mom was there and said, "Think about this. If [showbiz] is taking such a toll, is this something you really want to do?"'

CHAPTER 2:
THE FIVE CORNERS

OF A CIRCLE

'WE KNEW WHAT WE WANTED AND WE CONCENTRATED ON IT'

For a band who have received as much critical flak as 'N Sync, it is surprising to note that in many ways they did not satisfy the accepted criteria of the formulaic boy band. For one, they formed the group themselves, without auditions and without management or record company involvement. Unbeknown to Justin, his role in *The Mickey Mouse Club* would throw him into the unlikely set of events that led to the band being formed.

'N Sync first started to gel around Chris Kirkpatrick, who was ten years Justin's senior. Chris came from a Pennsylvanian family with numerous connections to the music business and inevitably he was soon heavily involved in the performing arts and music himself, in school plays, choirs and talent contests. This path took him to an Associates of Arts degree, and eventually on to sunny Orlando, Florida, where he funded his pop star dreams by working part time in various jobs, including vocal work for a carol group, before he eventually ended up at the Universal Studios theme park as a doo-wop performer.

Singing for a resort group called The Hollywood High Tones, Chris soon met Brooklyn-born Joey Fatone, six years his junior, himself the son of an original 1950s doo-wop singer and theatre producer. After a family relocation to Orlando, Joey also worked his way through school productions and musicals, appearing in Shakespeare's *Macbeth* and in a minor role in the 1993 film *Matinee*, plus another movie called *Once Upon a Time in America* and the TV show *Sea Quest*. Meanwhile, his brother Steven and sister Janine found work at the Universal Studios resort and, through this connection, Joey landed a role in the resort's *Beetlejuice Graveyard Revue*. Soon after he bumped into Chris Kirkpatrick.

As yet, Justin Timberlake was nowhere to be seen – but the random pieces of the 'N Sync jigsaw were slowly falling in to place. During his time on *The Mickey Mouse Club*, Justin had become close friends with presenter JC. They often spent their few spare hours singing with a vocal coach called Robin Wiley or at dance classes together. One choreographer/teacher in particular, Wade Robson, who had previously worked with both Michael Jackson and Prince, made a big impact on Justin's developing style. The duo even travelled to Nashville to work with other vocal coaches and writers. On their way back from one of these musical expeditions, the pair bumped into Chris Kirkpatrick at Universal Studios, who told them he was thinking of starting a band and that his friend, Joey Fatone, was already interested.

After a tip-off from Justin's Nashville vocal coach, the newly formed quartet cemented the band line-up by recruiting James Lansten Bass (nicknamed 'Lance'), a Mississippi-born aspiring actor from a deeply Christian southern states family. Immediately, they began rehearsing relentlessly, focusing special attention on their natural vocal harmonies. Their first song together was a sugary *a cappella* version of 'The Star-Spangled Banner'. Justin's mother, Lynn, suggested they take the last letter of each of their Christian names to create a word that also summed up their tight and melodious harmonies, hence their moniker: 'N Sync was born.

Outside in the big, scary world of the music business, there were signs that the public's ears were open to listening to pop music once more. The most obvious example was Tiffany, a teen star who enjoyed a huge, albeit brief, profile around the globe in the late '80s. Tiffany's management pioneered the art of targeting modern pop artists at youth audiences, most notably by playing tours in shopping malls. Unfortunately, Tiffany also found out that these same audiences were acutely fickle – within two years of the release of her worldwide smash single, 'I Think We're Alone Now', her records were failing to chart at all.

On a grander scale, there were two huge boy bands who provided ample inspiration for 'N Sync, namely New Kids On The Block and the Backstreet Boys. The former had ruled the world of music in 1989 and 1990, at one point posting the biggest-grossing ticket sales of all time for

their world tour. Their wealth was so vast that they regularly chartered aeroplanes to fly around the world for their sell-out tours. One of the charter airline companies they often used was run by businessman Lou Pearlman. After repeated bookings by NKOTB, Pearlman began to think that there was more money to be made managing boy bands than from managing their aeroplanes, and he decided to change his career entirely. His first effort at boy band management was the all-conquering Backstreet Boys.

Backstreet began their career in the mid-'90s, when the climate of the music biz was simply not suited to their pure-pop sound. Grunge had finally tailed off, but the long-haired slacker culture surrounding bands such as Nirvana, Pearl Jam and Soundgarden still threatened to suffocate any hopes of a pop revival. Add to this the huge popularity of gangster rap and hip-hop (acts such as Snoop Dogg, Dr Dre and the more mainstream Puff Daddy), and it meant that squeaky-clean, wholesome boy bands were really fighting against fashion. Most observers doubted the Backstreet Boys would even get on the radio.

Not only did they get on the radio – they ruled it. Their album sales were staggering, their live tours sold out huge arenas the world over,

and merchandise revenue ran into tens of millions of dollars. Backstreet were massive and in the process almost single-handedly made pop the most in-demand currency once more. The 31 million teenagers in America were said to have an estimated disposable income of $122 billion. It seems fair to suggest that the majority of these typical teenagers did not want to spend their free time listening to songs about heroin addiction.

By the time 'N Sync were soon to be breaking through barriers at MTV, mainstream radio and venues around the globe had already been primed by the awesome success of Backstreet. They couldn't take sole credit, of course – the omnipresent Spice Girls similarly broke down every anti-girl band obstacle they met. However, the biggest benefits to 'N Sync always came from the path beaten down by Backstreet.

Justin and the rest of 'N Sync were immediately thrown into a hectic professional lifestyle, working day jobs then rehearsing at night, sometimes until well after midnight. 'We didn't take it lightly,' recalled Justin. 'We knew what we wanted and we concentrated on it.' Asked to describe his fellow bandmates at this very early stage in their career, Justin said, 'Lance is the quiet one – he's a shy guy. JC's always moving – he has to be dancing around or doing something in the background. Chris is the smart alec and Joey's the guy with the wackiest clothing. And me, I'm just goofy. In a good way.'

At first, Lynn Harless's involvement in 'N Sync and her son's career did not stop at creating the embryonic band's name. She and her husband, Paul, effectively managed them through their early days (she has since stayed heavily involved throughout Justin's solo career, being credited as 'exclusive management for Just-In Time Entertainment' on the liner notes for *Justified*). However, the five boys would soon come into contact with the man behind the Backstreet Boys, the aforementioned music biz entrepreneur Louis Pearlman, now known as 'Big Poppa'. From now on, their lives would be changed forever.

Louis himself had been playing guitar since the age of eight and even had success in a rock–soul band which supported acts such as Donna Summer and Kool and the Gang. Thereafter, he attended Queens College, where Jerry Seinfeld was a classmate, and earned an MBA. Since turning his attention from his aviation business to managing the Backstreet Boys, Pearlman had become one of the most powerful music moguls in the world.

'N Sync had recorded a basic video demo with the help of an aspiring director friend, which they diligently mailed out to dozens of top management companies. It was this package that brought them to the attention of Pearlman.

Immediately impressed by their good looks and excellent vocals, Pearlman took 'N Sync under his seasoned wing. He has since likened having both 'N Sync and the Backstreet Boys to creating Coca-Cola and then Pepsi, and unfortunately his championing of the former eventually caused considerable animosity and disagreement with Backstreet, who felt they were being sidelined in favour of the newer act.

However, for now, Pearlman was manager of both bands and he quickly worked his magic by securing them a record deal with BMG Records in Europe. This was a strategy he had developed with Backstreet, who debuted their early singles, first album and initial tours on the continent. Thus, 'N Sync were sent across the Atlantic to start trawling around the diverse countries of Europe, to gain both live experience and overseas profile.

The demographic of these shows was very mixed, with 'N Sync complementing the traditional boy band fodder of under-sixteen school shows with some more courageous over-21 dates. They gigged relentlessly, in bars, in colleges, even in coffee shops. During these formative months, Justin rapidly learned how to work an audience, familiarised himself with the logistics of each stage show, learned to endure the rigours of touring and essentially took a crash course in the life of a pop star. He was still only fifteen.

The demanding, but carefully targeted, strategy worked so well that, within a few months, 'N Sync were one of the most hotly tipped boy bands surfacing in Europe. In between

SQUEAKY-CLEAN, WHOLESOME BOY BANDS WERE REALLY FIGHTING AGAINST FASHION

THEY GIGGED RELENTLESSLY, IN BARS, IN COLLEGES, EVEN IN COFFEE SHOPS

these tours, the boys would fly home to the USA to work on their forthcoming debut recorded output. Although 'N Sync's early music may not be the critics' favourite, the cleverly selected collaborations with big-name producers was a ploy that Justin would carry with him directly into his solo career. Hence, despite being relative unknowns, 'N Sync worked with a raft of mega-successful Europop producers, amongst them Sweden's Max Martin and the late, legendary Denniz Pop (who had worked with Robyn and Ace of Base, amongst others).

'N Sync's debut single, 'I Want You Back', was admittedly somewhat formulaic. The track smacked heavily of the Backstreet Boys' sound and even the band's look in the promo video was decidedly similar. Against such accusations of copying Backstreet, Justin was always happy to acknowledge their debt to the other Pearlman group and anxiously played down emerging rumours of interband rivalry. 'People try to make a feud out of everything,' said Justin to one reporter, 'and we didn't even see it like that.' Nevertheless, in the early stages of their career, 'N Sync were constantly gauged against the Backstreet Boys.

However, the thumpingly weird bass, sugary melodies and fierce dance beat of 'I Want You Back' made it a big hit on the pop-hungry dance floors of Europe, regardless of any comparisons with Backstreet. Sweden was the first country to send the track to number one and within weeks the same feat was achieved across much of the continent. 'N Sync were up and running.

At this point, the achingly young Justin Timberlake looked remarkably different from the ultra-cool fashionista that he'd grown into by the launch of his solo career. His teenage, wiry frame was a far cry from the toned, six-packed figure of later years. His hair was unusual, the naturally brown, curly texture dyed blonde and coated in thick gel, which held his locks tight on to his head in a French crop (he had a very brief and ill-advised flirtation with cornrows, but at least he didn't go so far as the laughable *Predator*-style black and white braids of Chris Kirkpatrick). Although his barnet was still far from model material, he was now quite at ease with his unconventional hair. 'You know, believe it or not, it takes me, like, two seconds to do my hair!' he said. 'I just dump some crap on it and it does

what it does. Lately it's just been, like, everywhere. I used to try to straighten my hair when I was younger and that was a big mistake! It just can't be done!'

His clothes consisted of a college boy mixture of US football/baseball caps and oversized shirts, brand name T-shirts and the occasional less-than-fetching white cotton vest. To top off the cheesy effect, he wore a gold necklace bearing the band's name and sported various earrings, ranging from simple studs or pirate hoops to top-of-the-ear piercings. Really early pictures show him sporting a multi-hoop wooden necklace *à la* female African warriors, but fortunately Justin got over this phase quite quickly.

The band's equally catchy second single, 'Tearin' Up My Heart', was confirmation that 'N Sync were capable of tapping into their own rich vein of pop standards. In Europe, it met with similar commercial success and primed the continent perfectly for the band's debut album, simply called *'N Sync*.

'N Sync's first album was predictable but polished pop, veering little from the course set by their two previous singles (both included here). The seductive sounds of 'Giddy Up' and

the pacey 'Here We Go' at least showcased their impressive vocal harmonies, as did the sickly sweet 'God Must Have Spent A Little More Time On You'. Seamlessly mixing pure pop with gentle ballads, snatches of notable *a cappella* and – the only real surprise – odd smatterings of R&B, this was an unadventurous but obviously winning formula. Rather oddly, they also covered Bread's 'Everything I Own' and Christopher Cross's 'Sailing'. Although filtered through 'N Sync's shameless pop vision, the band openly paid tribute to their influences including Sting, Boyz II Men, Brian McKnight and Garth Brooks among others. Justin's preference for R&B weighed heavily on these debut album sessions. Although he was not writing any material at this stage, the presence of his CDs on the tour bus and the subsequent influence of his record collection on his own vocals had already started to make an indelible impression on 'N Sync's musical evolution.

Europe quickly fell under the spell of the debut album, but already thoughts were turning to the band's native USA. As yet, they had – deliberately – not toured or released any material over there and, despite his heartthrob status across the pond, Justin could walk down any

Supporting them on these exciting 'N Sync dates was a young, southern pop singer who was already very familiar to JC and Justin – the then unknown Britney Spears. Justin's future girlfriend was still an all-American sweetheart at this stage and made no secret that she was embarrassed by the female attention her old friend JT was getting on the road. 'Oh my Gosh, you should see these screaming girls. It's unreal, I mean, the things they do to see [him] is unbelievable . . . I've been out there and girls out in the audience are lifting their shirts up, and I'm dying. I'm like, "Oh my goodness, I'm not believing this. This is bad."'

At first, 'N Sync's debut album was only available in America in its imported European version. Once Pearlman secured the band a record deal with RCA, however, momentum really began to gather. Gradually, sales figures for the indigenous debut album began creeping up, helped by extra bonus tracks not on the imported version.

The boys had been deeply embroiled in this exhaustive schedule for months and months when their manager told them that their record sales were beginning to explode. One week in mid-August 1998 saw over a quarter of a million copies of 'N Sync sold in just five days! The momentum gained by the live shows, expanding teen magazine coverage and massive radio play was such that the rise up the charts was unstoppable. Later that summer, the boys received the news that their record had finally climbed to number one in the Billboard charts. By way of celebration, the whole band – except Joey – had tattoos inked in their skin.

Further singles from the album boosted the already impressive sales: eventually 'N Sync had produced four US Number 1 hits: 'I Want You Back', 'Tearin' Up My Heart', 'God Must Have Spent A Little More Time On You' and 'Drive Myself Crazy'. Only six months after its US release, 'N Sync passed the platinum mark of one million copies sold in that country alone. But the success didn't stop there: if anything it accelerated. A year later, the debut record passed the incredible

street in any American town completely unnoticed. Not for long.

'N Sync's attack on the United States was driven by the same tactic as that which had worked so well in Europe – sheer relentless touring. Critics are quick to denigrate boy bands, but the simple fact is that most teen bands play far more live shows than so-called 'credible' acts.

With Pearlman's extensive contacts and leverage within the US music industry, one of 'N Sync's earliest American tours was supporting Janet Jackson on her extensive *Velvet Rope* jaunt (a lady with whom Justin would later come to have an altogether different relationship in 2002). They also supported the gaggle of rough diamonds that made up British boy band Five, and then shared the stage with the somewhat more sophisticated Jordan Knight on the *Boys Of Summer* tour.

'N Sync toured mercilessly, covering thousands of miles in the promotion of their record. The groundswell of fans in their native country slowly but surely started to merge with news of their profile in Europe, such that they were soon in a position to start going out on their own headline dates.

global sales mark of 10 million copies. In the process, Justin and his band joined a very élite clique of artists who had achieved this, such as Whitney Houston, Elton John and Madonna. Yet more European tours, as well as sold-out dates in Mexico, the Far East and South Africa, cemented 'N Sync's position as one of the world's premier pop acts.

In light of Justin's latter-day profile as an über-cool R&B/hip-hop maestro, it is all the more remarkable to reflect on some of the records 'N Sync chose to release. For any other artist ultimately in search of street kudos, being involved in a Christmas-themed album would be a sure-fire course for self-destruction. However, it seems to matter not one iota to JT's credibility that he was involved in 'N Sync's nauseating festive album, *Home For Christmas*.

Agreed, the work demands of recording this seasonal slice of 'N Sync were severe, coming on top of their already prolific schedule on the road. However, sweat alone does not make a great record. Predictably cheesy, *Home For Christmas* was a creative abomination but a commercial mammoth. With their debut album still selling thousands of copies every day, 'N Sync recorded this cheerful, if not classic, collection of Christmas standards and brand new seasonal songs, including versions of 'The First Noel', 'Holy Night', 'Will You Be Mine This Christmas?' and 'In Love On Christmas'. At the time, Justin was as enthusiastic as any member of the band. 'Christmas carols are just so beautiful,' he merrily told an eager media. 'They're just pretty melodies, you know?'

Admittedly uncharitable critical reservations aside, this album was a huge commercial success, of course, giving 'N Sync two albums in the Billboard top ten simultaneously. Musically, it remains an album that Justin probably chooses to file at the very back of his personal record collection. Still, the numerous *a cappella* songs and many harmonies (in one instance, on 'O Holy Night', there is a total of seven) did at least showcase the band's growing vocal prowess.

All this time, despite the fact that 'N Sync were very much the newest (and youngest) gang in town, the media spotlight was increasingly falling on Justin. In interviews, journalists fired all their questions at him while the rest of the band often sat in silence. At times, they even likened themselves to the band No Doubt – such was the isolated focus the media placed on singer Gwen Stefani that the band had to prohibit magazine cover shoots unless all four members were included. For 'N Sync, the problem was not as severe as this but, if nothing else, it was definitely an indication that the media and public alike found something intriguing about the young Mr Timberlake.

One of the main reasons why the interviewer's gaze most often fell on Justin was the swelling rumour that he and his former *Mickey Mouse Club* cohort Britney Spears were becoming more than just good friends. At first, such whispers were flatly and vehemently denied by both parties.

Undeterred, 'N Sync ploughed on with their unforgiving schedule. When they played their very own Disney Special, and shortly afterwards sold out five consecutive nights at the famous Radio City Music Hall in New York, it confirmed that Justin was the front man of the world's biggest pop band. Their next album would take their success – and with it Justin's own profile – on to a completely different level altogether.

CHAPTER 3:

FINALLY COMING K

Industry observers were surprised by the strength of the sales of 'N Sync's first two albums, perhaps especially the festive offering. However, no one could have foreseen what was about to happen next. Having almost immediately plunged back into the recording studio after the success of 'N Sync, the band were ready to capitalise on the colossal groundswell of support their records and prolific touring had generated.

This time, however, there was an important development in the studio for the third album, to be called *No Strings Attached*. Gone was the pop whitewash and instead in came a growing palate of styles, with R&B rifling strongly through the sessions. Again, Justin was at the forefront of this progression and was personally delighted to be working with songwriters such as Diane Warren and Babyface (radio-friendly star Richard Marx was also recruited to keep the pop flavours ever present). The band also insisted on delaying the production so that they could work with She'kspere and there are also tracks with Teddy Riley and Riprock, as well as the late Lisa 'Left Eye' Lopes of TLC.

Like Justin's future solo album, the production on the record was exquisite, regardless of whether the songs were your flavour or not. It was an extremely modern record, layering the tracks with synthesisers, strings, harmonised vocals and fantastic beats, while all the time drawing in (highly) diluted touches of R&B, hip-hop, jazz and more traditional balladry. There were even splashes of techno in the band's more up-tempo dance numbers. Even more alternative stars were moved to acknowledge the record's composition, such as Moby, who told *Spin*, 'So much effort has gone into this you almost have to like it. You have twenty Swedish guys writing the songs, and they know what they're doing. It's the craft aspect – like looking at a well put together cabinet. You may not want to buy the cabinet, but you can be impressed by how well its doors open.'

The obvious first single from *No Strings Attached* was the punchy 'Bye, Bye, Bye', which Justin was happy to see drag the band towards a harder edge: 'We needed something for us guys because (TLC's) "No Scrubs" came out and (Destiny's Child's) "Bills, Bills, Bills" came out, and it was all dissing guys.' The funky, future US number one single, 'It's Gonna Be Me', was similarly themed. Elsewhere, fans were not disappointed by the smooth vocals and lush ballads, ranging

GONE WAS THE POP WHITEWASH AND IN CAME A GROWING PALATE OF STYLES

from covers, such as Johnny Kemp's 1988 hit 'Just Got Paid', and original material, like the Marx-composed 'This I Promise You'. Themes of fame, its price and consequences sat comfortably next to the band's more orthodox chronicles of emotional relationships.

In light of Justin's solo career, this record was most notable for the progression towards writing his own material. The band co-wrote many of the songs and Justin was reported to be busying himself behind the mixing desk, watching the engineers at work. It was the perfect moment to start delving deeper into the studio mechanics. Overall, although it was never going to win over the alternative music fans, *No Strings Attached* contained many promising signs that 'N Sync were starting to mutate into something altogether more intriguing.

On a sadder note, it was during this time that the band parted company with Lou Pearlman and RCA Records. Multimillion-dollar lawsuits and counter lawsuits followed, until the difficult period was eventually settled out of court. In the aftermath, the band instead moved to Jive Records, home of Britney Spears. However, the scars had cut deep. 'It was hell and I was really discouraged,' Justin

later told *The Face*. 'It's the only time in my life where I looked at what I was doing and I was like, "I don't wanna do this no more." That was a real lesson for me.' Ever since this legal tussle, Justin has maintained a merciless grip on every aspect of his career, with the able and constant assistance of his mother, Lynn.

The company Soundscan have been keeping accurate records of American album sales since 1991 and the prestigious accolades of fastest-selling records make fascinating reading. For a long time the grunge classic *Versus*, the second album by Eddie Vedder's Pearl Jam, had held the top slot with just under one million sales in a week. That was an incredible achievement in itself. Then Garth Brooks's *Double Live* album shifted an awesome 1,085,373 copies in seven days, followed swiftly after by the Backstreet Boys' rather brilliant *Millennium* record, which sold 100,000 more than Brooks. These figures were huge and few felt that Backstreet's record would be substantially improved upon for many years, if ever.

Then 'N Sync released *No Strings Attached*. In short, the sales records were obliterated. The Backstreet Boys' impressive first-week record was almost beaten in one day with *No Strings* shifting 1.13 million units in ten working hours. That

represents two thousand records sold per minute. The success did not stop there, with each day racking up hundreds of thousands more sales, finally peaking at the week's end with an unbelievable total of 2.4 million units, well over twice the previous record. This made *No Strings Attached* the first album ever to sell more than two million copies in its first week of release.

Previously sceptical industry observers watched in amazement. The signs had been there with the huge sales of the January 2000 single 'Bye, Bye, Bye', but nobody had expected this level of popularity. The insiders who had sneered at the band's failure to win either of the two Grammys they had been nominated for now looked rather foolish.

As if these figures weren't impressive enough, 'N Sync set out on a mammoth tour of 52 US dates and scores more across the globe. By now, 'N Sync's success in the US had been replicated all over the world, with the Far East, South America, Australia and their original fan-base in Europe all being visited. Some desperate female fans even lived in a dumpster for a week to try to win front row seats to one of their New York shows.

The figures for the *No Strings Attached* tour made similarly mind-boggling reading as the actual record sales. In one single day, their native tour sold out, shifting over $40 million worth of tickets within eight working hours. To service these shows, the boys needed twelve buses, nineteen trucks and a budget of about $1.1 million per show. At the shows themselves, the band brought back memories of The Beatles' fans' hysteria when the volume of screaming was so high that, on medical advice, 'N Sync were forced to wear ear-pieces to avoid permanent damage to their hearing.

Justin seemed almost shell-shocked by the mounting scale of their success. 'We know people are out there [but] we're a little nervous about the expectations people have,' he said. Interestingly, for these dates the dance routines Justin performed were becoming increasingly complex while his solo spots and sequences seemed to reinforce the

'IT WAS HELL AND I WAS REALLY DISCOURAGED'

growing suspicion that here was a true solo star in the making.

'N Sync were not just a big boy band, in keeping with the tradition of artists targeting younger audiences, but they were also a commercially colossal brand. Just like the Spice Girls, the Backstreet Boys, NKOTB and generations of young bands before them, 'N Sync released countless items of merchandise that were eagerly snapped up by obsessive fans. Thus we had the usual suspects on the store shelves such as 'N Sync T-shirts, badges, posters, hats, a board game, dolls, and even lip balm (Justin's flavour was vanilla)!

Their website was declared the most popular music site in the world, with nearly one million hits a month. More exotically, the Caribbean islands of St Vincent and the Grenadines even issued stamps featuring the band members' profiles, making them among the few countries who allow living people to appear on their stamps. The Postmaster of St Vincent said she chose 'N Sync because the band 'represented the best of what art and entertainment can present to young people, as they are positive role models with a positive message'. 'N Sync also took part in two of America's biggest institutions, namely by singing at the Super Bowl and making a cameo appearance on *The Simpsons*. The result of all this success was that in 2000, 'N Sync grossed over $267 million in album and tour sales alone. In business terms, this effectively classified them as a medium-sized corporation.

The commercial juggernaut that *No Strings Attached* had become did not finish after one week, either – they soon notched up the highest sales for the first five weeks (5 million copies,

compared with Backstreet's 1.4 million for *Millennium*); highest figures for two months (8 million); and the quickest ever achievement of platinum sales of 10 million. To give this feat some more recent perspective, the all-conquering Eminem was considered by most to be the biggest artist in the world at the turn of the Millennium. Even so, initial sales of his three studio albums and one soundtrack album, although huge, fell dramatically short of the historical benchmark set by *No Strings Attached*. It is now widely regarded that 'N Sync's sales record for this album is unlikely ever to be beaten.

Although 'N Sync were a five-piece band, the staggering commercial success of *No Strings Attached* meant that Justin's personal profile had never been higher. One specific reason why JT was the clear focus of 'N Sync, apart from his obvious dancing and vocal ability, was the growing speculation about his love life. As mentioned before, it was no secret that he was a close friend of Britney Spears, but with her own pop career about to go nuclear with the release of her debut single, 'Hit Me Baby (One More Time)', the media spotlight on this possible pairing intensified.

Apart from the tour dates when Britney supported Justin's band, the pair were often spotted at each other's separate gigs. The tabloids picked up on the theme and installed them as the latest celebrity couple to watch. Even though Britney was barely into her own solo career, she was soon voted second in *People* magazine's website list of 'Most Beautiful People of 1999', beaten only by . . . Justin Timberlake, the cream of the crop.

JUSTIN'S PERSONAL PROFILE HAD NEVER BEEN HIGHER

At first, Britney strongly denied any romance, saying, 'No, it's not true. They're (all) just like big brothers to me. I guess that's why they think that, because we were on *The Mickey Mouse Club* together, so they just assume that.' For his part, Justin said, 'This has really gotten out of hand; me and Britney are not dating, much less getting married. I have said this many times before and I will say it again, we are friends, nothing more. We hang out, yes, and we do fly out sometimes to catch each other's shows and we hook up while in the same city but we are not a couple.'

Undeterred, the tabloids kept digging, however. Claims circulated that the two were sharing a $3,000-a-month apartment (much to the surprise of their parents!) and were possibly even engaged. Chat show host Jay Leno added to the interest by joking that if they did get married, it would be the only wedding in history where both bride and groom lip-synched their wedding vows. The British tabloid *News of the World* was at the very centre of these rumours and announced that Justin chose the less-than-romantic setting of a stool in a coffee bar to propose, whipping out a $50,000 ring among the frappuccinos and lattes.

Later, when Britney missed an autograph signing session, rumours swirled that she was staying with JT. All this speculation forced Jive Records (home to both Britney and 'N Sync) to release an official statement aimed at quelling the escalating rumours. It said; 'Contrary to what has been erroneously reported, Britney Spears and Justin Timberlake are neither engaged nor married. The story . . . is, not surprisingly, completely without merit.' There was a sinister side to this press intrusion, however; the low point came when a totally fictitious news item announced that Britney had been killed and Justin was in a coma after a car crash. Members of both stars' families were left unsure if this horrible story was true for several harrowing hours.

Why would two attractive young pop stars be at such pains to deny any romance? One obvious reason for such secrecy was that for both male and female pop stars, declaring a partner in public can be the death knell of a career. Since rock and roll began in the 1950s, part of the allure of following a particular star has been that minuscule, million-to-one chance that somehow the celebrity in question will see past all the seductive A-list beauties and millions of other fans desperate for their affections and chose you as their lover. Ridiculous, maybe, but that is the fantasy that has sold hundreds of millions of records and funds the careers of the majority of pop stars. The same cloak-and-dagger approach can also surround a gay boy band star – if your favourite hunk has the temerity to have a girlfriend, at least he may dump her. But if he doesn't even fancy girls in the first place . . . Very few pop stars have the courage to come out as gay early in their career, *Pop Idol* Will Young being one notable and laudable exception.

Both Britney and Justin had ulterior motives for keeping any relationship quiet. JT was happy to answer questions about his ideal girlfriend and keep his legions of fans hoping and wondering; 'I look for honesty and sensitivity, someone with a sense of humour,' he told *Bop!* magazine. 'And I like independence. It's like she's her own woman, her own person. She's a girl who speaks her mind

and takes charge of situations. Oh, and I really dig girls who are into basketball!'

Eventually, it became public knowledge that the two were indeed an item after all. It appears that the pair just got tired of all the speculation. Britney was the first to make a move towards admitting the affair, when she told *Rolling Stone* in May 2000 that they did indeed kiss, a declaration which was followed by an exasperated gasp of 'Oh my gosh, my manager is going to kill me!' Justin seemed relieved, a suspicion confirmed when he later admitted these denials were one of the career moves that had most plagued him with guilt. The trouble was, with his relationship now out in the open, the media inquisitiveness stepped up a gear rather than tailing off as they had hoped it would. Matters became all the more embarrassing with the nature of the relationship itself. Males all over the world could not help but feel for Justin when Britney proceeded to emphasise shamelessly how she would absolutely, definitely remain a virgin until her wedding night.

By now, of course, Justin was a very wealthy man. Before he had sold a single solo album, he was reputed to be worth over £30 million, much of that having been earned in his teens. He was a bona fide A-list celebrity and with that

came the whole lifestyle: the cars, the mansion, the film premieres, but also, and increasingly so, the invasion of privacy and at times the sheer weirdness of it all.

The same could be said for 'N Sync as a unit. The problem many huge bands face is that their creativity becomes a victim of its own success. Their first album or two are created out of their struggle to break through, usually written around very personal themes or experiences. Then, if not by the second album then certainly by the third, a band's sphere of experience is no longer what 'normal' people endure: nine-to-five jobs, paying bills, the minutiae of life and so on. A successful band coming up to their second or third album will have probably spent most of the last two or three years on a tour bus, cocooned from the outside world by bodyguards and VIP treatment. They will have little or no experience of life outside the protective bubble of the band. Their professional infrastructure will by now be filled with 'yes' men and women. Their grasp of reality, for all but the most grounded of personalities, can drift away very easily.

Most bands inevitably end up writing about what it is like to be in a band. The problem with this is that it creates material that is self-indulgent and appealing to the minute minority of the population who are also band members. History shows us that The Beatles, The Monkees, David Cassidy, The Bay City Rollers, and more recent boy bands such as New Kids On The Block have

'I LOOK FOR HONESTY AND SENSITIVITY, SOMEONE WITH A SENSE OF HUMOUR'

all done it. By contrast, The Backstreet Boys and Take That chose to explore this route in a more positive way, writing songs about their fans. However, this development is often a sign that a band is running out of themes to write about or – more worryingly – is about to split up. So it was with some trepidation that critics reacted to the news that 'N Sync's fourth studio album would be a concept piece entitled *Celebrity*.

In the official statement preceding the release of the record, Justin said, 'We chose the title *Celebrity* because the term is a misconception of what people really are.' He also teased fans about the record's content, telling *Rolling Stone*, 'I didn't think it was going to be this crazy, something keeps happening every time we put an album together that this vibe kinda kicks in. It's so intense but it's a hell of a lot of fun.' The sleeve for the record was refreshingly self-deprecating, which at least meant the band were approaching this prickly subject with their tongues planted firmly in their cheeks.

Fortunately, the band had evolved enough musically to pull off this rather risqué project. The album *Celebrity* was a surprisingly accomplished take on the absurdities of life as a pop star, a central theme which was wisely coupled

with the band's more usual musings on love, life and relationships. The band coined the phrase 'dirty pop' to describe their music and their predicament (also a lyric used in forthcoming single 'Pop'), and after listening to Celebrity, who was to argue?

The central chunk of the new record was sophisticated pop, steering clear of too much musical diversion, but nonetheless delivering top drawer pure pop with a twist. Future Grammy-nominated single 'Pop' and the record's title track were the best cases in point. 'Just Don't Tell Me' was a simple boy–girl scenario plainly told. More familiar 'N Sync territory cropped up with the Max Martin tracks 'Tell Me, Tell Me . . . Baby' and 'Just Don't Tell Me That'. There were richly orchestrated ballads too, such as 'Gone' (strings courtesy of The Hampton String Quartet; beatbox courtesy of JT), but this was neatly counterpointed by the much raunchier 'Up Against The Wall', masterminded by cool remixers Riprock 'n' Alex G.

The track 'Something Like You' brought JT into contact with one of his childhood heroes, Stevie Wonder, who played harmonica on the tune. The problem was, on the day of recording both JT and the producer felt the final note by Mr Wonder was out of tune. Neither wanted to

tell the living legend to try again, but eventually Justin plucked up the courage. He pressed the talkback button to the booth and apprehensively told Wonder. As soon as he had finished his sentence, he winced and quickly took his finger off the button, turning to his studio cohorts to say, 'I just told Stevie Wonder he's out of tune. I'm going straight to hell!' It later transpired that the harmonica, and not Wonder, was out of tune.

The Pacman themed track 'Game Is Over' revealed the band's more experimental side – an acerbic pop song for sure, but one which cleverly used arcade game noises as a percussive back-beat. Likewise, the magnificent 'Pop', on first listen, sounds like a sure-fire radio pop hit, yet, on further inspection, is actually a heavily produced mini-masterpiece. Produced by underground doyen Brian 'BT' Transeau, this beat-driven song was dripping with layered sounds, studio effects and myriad intricately synergised vocals. The track seemed almost a deliberate precursor to Justin's solo album. Most obviously, the final beatbox close-out to the song, performed by Justin alone in the band's multimillion-pound video for this track, could have been straight out of *Justified*.

However, it was with tracks such as another future single, 'Girlfriend', that the breadth of the band's vision really began to unfold and consequently the groundwork for JT's solo career continued to be laid. 'Girlfriend' was another lovers' song, yet it was so much more than that in terms of where 'N Sync were heading. Produced by the Neptunes and Rodney Jerkins, its addictive guitar strumming and funky back-beats made it the band's biggest venture into R&B territory yet.

The vocals were highly inventive, with snatches of the falsetto backing and voice-versus-instrument trade-offs that would later become such an instant trademark of Justin's solo work. The accompanying Marc Klasfield-directed video for the single was to prove prophetic for JT's future solo image too, with the crowd scenes of dancing and hanging out, the car racing and generally much more funky appearance of all the band, not just Justin. Both this track and 'Gone' enjoyed much crossover airplay on urban radio, laying crucial foundations for Justin's future R&B-drenched solo album.

As an aside, the videos for both 'Girlfriend' and 'Pop' showed that by now Justin's style had evolved enormously from the rather cheesy first press photos of his 'N Sync career. Gone was the curly hair, replaced by a grade one shaven skull. In came fashionably faded jeans, label trainers and a 'JT' necklace. He was starting to look like a model from a Times Square billboard. Not by coincidence, the fashion mags and style publications were also starting to take more notice of him. He was growing up in front of our very eyes.

When both 'Pop' and 'Girlfriend' became huge hits, the path to a solo career seemed to have been opened up for Justin by his very own band. The reasons behind this were simple enough – Justin was heavily involved in the album's writing and production work. The band was working with some of the most highly sought-after producers and mixers in the business, such as Rodney Jenkins, Brian McKnight and, notably for Justin, Pharrell Williams and the Neptunes. Alongside these eminent names on *Celebrity*, Justin co-wrote seven tracks and co-produced five. Most of these

were created with Wade J Robson, who was actually the band's revered choreographer. Justin was so convinced that he and Wade were on the same wavelength that he approached the latter about working together on the music too, which proved to be a very productive and insightful suggestion: they came up with 'Pop', 'Celebrity', 'See Right Through You' and 'Gone'.

Commercially, it was perhaps no surprise that *Celebrity* was yet another huge smash. The record-breaking first-week sales of *No Strings Attached* couldn't be matched, but this was still a multimillion-selling album – in fact, its 1,879,955 first-week sales in the US made it the second fastest-selling album of all time behind *No Strings Attached*. Similarly, the world tour for the album, called *Pop Odyssey*, with its pyrotechnics and extravagant stage sets, sold out stadiums across the globe.

More pleasingly for the band, perhaps, critics warmed to the experimental flavour of the new album and people seemed genuinely open to 'N Sync reinventing themselves as a more mature and credible vocal group, rather than a predictable boy band of limited scope. This was best exemplified by the Grammy nominations for both the album and two songs from the project, 'Gone' and 'Girlfriend' (for 'Best Pop Vocal Album', and 'Best Pop Performance By A Duo Or Group With Vocal' in 2002 and 2003 respectively). Justin was pleased with this development, saying, 'Call us what you want. Call us the first real boy band, if you want. Just don't disrespect the fact that we're musicians. We're not just trying to sell T-shirts, you know?'

The naysayers quickly pointed out that 'N Sync were still a manufactured band and therefore had no validity or relevance to music history. This was nonsense, of course. OK, so 'N Sync may not be cited as equal reference points to the Fab Four in thirty years' time, but for starters they were not actually manufactured. As previously mentioned, they formed the band themselves, then found management. They even gigged relentlessly – more than 250 shows in one calendar year, a record even Bruce Springsteen would be proud of.

Critical scepticism perennially highlights a litany of reasons why boy bands like 'N Sync are risible: their apparent lack of songwriting (Elvis or Cliff anyone?); their frequent recruitment through auditions (NME Classifieds?); their clichéd 'roles' or personalities, notoriously a boyish

All-black female groups dominated much of the 1960s charts, by which time it was long overdue for the men to enter the market – The Monkees were perhaps the most clear case of a manufactured male band, recruited for a television show, with music that was not played by the band members but which did not lessen their huge popularity. Later boy band incarnations have included acts such as The Osmonds, The Bay City Rollers, Bros and even Wham! The modern incarnation was epitomised by the global corporation that the aforementioned New Kids On The Block became, at one point the biggest-grossing act on the planet for three consecutive years. Smaller, but nevertheless enormous, success was also enjoyed by Bros, Take That, Boyzone and countless others. Yet still the

THE BAND WERE ALL OPENLY RELIGIOUS

one, a wacky one, a dull-but-good-at-music one, a dancing one and an older one for the mums (what about 'proper' bands with the moody bassist, the 'mad' drummer, egotistical lead singer and 'mastermind' guitarist?); the constant managerial input (Peter Grant, Brian Epstein . . .); the expensive videos (Michael Jackson, P Diddy etc.); and manufactured band members' eventual ventures into far less successful solo careers (The Beatles, Queen, The Rolling Stones?). Apparently, boy bands have 'not paid their dues' and know nothing of real pressure. Yet, when the prolific touring band the Backstreet Boys' *Black and Blue* album sold only eight million copies, whispers of a 'flop' bizarrely began to circulate.

These same critics also seem to ignore the fact that so-called 'manufactured' bands are a vital part of music history. Few sectors of the music industry attract so much scorn yet fewer still sell as many records. All-female jazz and dance bands had existed since the 1920s.

snipers fired insults. Even other artists joined in. Most notably, Eminem filmed a parody of 'N Sync for one of his own videos; Blink 182 did the same with The Backstreet Boys.

And let's not forget 'charidee', mate. 'N Sync support numerous causes which have used their (artistically valid or not) celebrity to raise millions of dollars. Justin personally supported several children's charities and even established The Justin Timberlake Foundation, a music education awareness programme, which in May 2000 awarded its first grant to Justin's old elementary school, E.E. Jeeter, back in Tennessee. Justin has been honoured by the White House for the role his foundation has played in improving music education in public schools. Justin told the *New York Post* his motivation for this, 'I remember my parents always saying, "Remember your roots. Whatever happens, remember your roots, remember where you came from", and that's what I'm doing now. I want to give back to

the communities.' Some of the funds for this foundation have been raised by celebrity basketball matches, which Justin organises with other members of 'N Sync. Tragically, one of his fans was killed by a drunk driver while waiting to meet Justin outside a radio station. After this shocking event, Justin happily agreed to act as a spokesman for an anti-drunk driving campaign.

Although 'N Sync's record-breaking success was doing wonders for Justin's bank account, there were reservations that he would ever be able to break out and become a serious solo star. There were many elements of 'N Sync that surely could become a millstone for Justin's potential solo credibility. For one, the band were all openly religious, Lance particularly so. The latter had a cherished book which he carried with him at all times, *What Would Jesus Do?* Each of the boys had their own bracelets with the initials 'WWJD?' engraved on them. Rock and roll! In 1999 they were invited to perform on a CD being released by none other than Pope John Paul II, containing samples of his prayers. Pop Houdini he may be, but let's see the newly cool Justin Timberlake get that on the front cover of *Vibe*.

CHAPTER 4:
TAKE IT FROM HERE

Aside from the massive commercial success of 'N Sync's latest album and his increasing public profile, Justin was fast approaching the biggest period of change in his young life. His relationship with Britney Spears had been out in the open for a long time, so when it began to be suggested that the two were having problems, the media interest was predictably frenzied.

There was talk of Britney allegedly being unfaithful. Worse still, repeated rumours pointed to Wade Robson, Justin's friend and choreographer, an accusation that Robson vehemently denied. For weeks everybody was uncertain of their status, just as it had been when they first denied they were together. Eventually, both artists started asking journalists not to put forward questions about their private lives. Then, in March 2002, during a press conference for her debut feature film *Crossroads*, Britney admitted to the press pack that she was not 'in an intense relationship with anyone'. Yet, as late as the release of *Celebrity*, Justin was still clearly very close to Britney, leaving a gushing love message on the sleeve notes to 'Pinky', his affectionate name for her. So what had gone wrong?

It is easy to forget that they were both only just out of their teens. They led very hectic and bizarre lifestyles. They were both constantly attracting attention. Their schedules rarely allowed them much time together. Unfortunately, the general consensus seemed to be that Britney might have been unfaithful. Typically, there was no single prime suspect – as well as Robson being mentioned, there was even talk of Jennifer Lopez's future fiancé, Ben Affleck. None of these suggestions were substantiated.

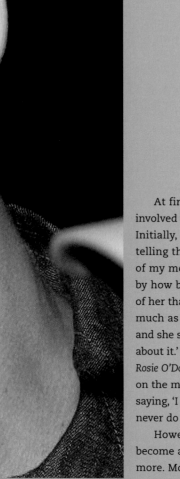

At first, Justin steadfastly refused to get involved in any backstabbing and recrimination. Initially, he seemed to be defending Britney, telling the *New York Daily News* that, 'outside of my mother, I've never been so impressed by how big [someone's] heart is. I see the side of her that others don't see. To be picked on as much as she is . . . and get hurt by what's said, and she still goes out there without really thinking about it.' When he appeared on the high profile *Rosie O'Donnell Show* in April 2002, and was pressed on the matter, he was once again evasive, simply saying, 'I love Britney with all my heart and I will never do anything to disrespect her.'

However, over the coming weeks, it did become apparent that the relationship was no more. Moreover, it appeared that Britney was anxious to get her love life with JT back on track. In the aftermath of the split, Britney made several attempts at reconciliation, but Justin did not appear interested.

As if to remind her of what she had lost, Justin was then voted 'America's Most Eligible Bachelor of the Year' in *People* magazine, which, among other things, cited his reputed £35 million personal fortune and $8 million home in the Hollywood Hills as two possible attractions. Visions of Justin driving to the golf course in his $100,000 Mercedes in order to practise his ten handicap must have filled a million women's dreams.

Although he owned such an incredible house in LA, during these difficult times, Justin spent many weeks back at his childhood home in Memphis. The Harless family still lived there, despite the millions of pounds Justin has since earned. They love it, he loves it and no one wanted

to move. At times like this, he found the familiarity and family atmosphere consoling. Besides, another seismic change was about to happen in his life: his solo career was about to be launched.

The possibility of a solo career for Justin Timberlake had been mooted by outsiders for some time. Initially, 'N Sync denied that any of their members were interested in new musical projects other than for the band. They openly courted film projects, even going so far as to visit the 53rd Cannes International Film Festival in France to talk up their own possible movie project. The official line was that, while 'N Sync were still so popular, no solo careers were planned.

However, the evidence suggested otherwise. JC had been working in the studio, particularly on soundtracks, most notably for material used in *The Grinch* starring Jim Carrey; Chris Kirkpatrick was looking into launching his own fashion range, to be named FuManSkeeto; Joey Fatone was talking up a movie based around Superman and then in 2003 accepted a role in a Broadway production of *Rent*; most bizarrely, Lance Bass had made it known that he was determined to become the first pop star in space, aboard a Russian rocket, but had yet to find the reputed $20 million fee. Even Justin was said to have been receiving countless movie scripts, including one asking him to play Clark Kent's sidekick Jimmy Olsen in the new *Superman* film.

The last tour date for *Celebrity*, in Orlando on 29 April 2002 (bizarrely supported by P Diddy), was even rumoured to be the band's last ever gig. Yet, a band spokeswoman denied rumours of an 'N Sync split, saying they were simply taking 'a little hiatus as they have not had one day off in five years,' adding that 'they should be back together by 2003'.

Unswayed, the media were convinced that changes were afoot. Justin was quickly established as the bookies' favourite to benefit the most. Take this extract from the *San Francisco Chronicle*: 'While it's a tiresome truth that every band's blond gets the most attention, JC, Lance, Chris and Joey probably also suspect what Elton John already knows: that when the teen-pop phenomenon has burned itself to the ground, their boy Curly will rise from its ashes like a hot buttered phoenix.'

However, what hopes were there for a successful solo career for Justin Timberlake? After all, wasn't he the one out of 'N Sync with the weird curly hair and a beautiful girlfriend who wouldn't let him sleep with her? In the UK at least, his profile up to this point was a fraction of the size of Britney's, although in the USA his mammoth record sales, albeit as part of a band, were clearly a superb foundation.

There were signs that he might be met with a positive critical reception – as far back as September 2000, with 'N Sync at the peak of their squeaky-clean, boy band life, the respected hip-hop/R&B chronicle *Vibe* magazine called for him to go solo, saying, 'He can sing, dance, and not many white boys can rock a curly, dirty-blond afro, much less cornrows, as well as he can.' Throughout 2001 there had been much speculation on the internet in chat rooms and message boards that JT was about to leave 'N Sync. Yet, as late as April 2002 (his *Justified* album would be released in November of that year), 'N Sync's record company Jive were denying reports of a solo album. Other critics were also more cautionary, noting that jumping out of a successful boy band and into a respected and lengthy solo career was never a foregone conclusion.

Historically, the odds are against a solo career for a former band member. In the UK, not one of the top one hundred bestselling singles by newly 'solo' stars outsold records by the groups they had left. Even George Michael, who did manage to establish himself as an award-winning solo star, could not outsell Wham! in the singles market at least.

Trawling back through time, The Beatles struggled to surpass their historic group sales. Likewise for The Rolling Stones and The Who.

A RESPECTED AND LENGTHY SOLO CAREER WAS NEVER A FOREGONE CONCLUSION

Stephen Gately sank almost without trace. Similarly, the Backstreet Boys' Nick Carter released his own solo album in 2003 to scathing critical disdain and very modest sales.

It seems the biggest solo stars start off as solo stars: Madonna, Prince, Janet Jackson, Whitney Houston, Mariah Carey, Shania Twain and so on. True, Michael Jackson was a former band member turned living legend, but his circumstances were so unique it is impossible to use them as any kind of reference or gauge for future aspiring solo careers (although Jacko played a pivotal part of Justin's solo work – more of which later).

So how did Justin Timberlake pull it off? How did he leave the sanctuary of the shockingly successful commercial behemoth that was 'N Sync and emerge unscathed with a critically revered reputation and multimillion sales? It is a remarkable achievement that principally revolved around one central facet: stunning music.

By the summer of 2002, the mystery surrounding Justin's solo plans had evaporated. His own 'insiders' were talking the project up, saying, 'Justin wants to go solo in every part of his life. He wants to be a bachelor, and he's looking forward to doing his own album.' JT worked on most of the album through the summer of 2002, travelling around the USA working with all the different producers, writers and other key figures he had carefully selected. He was suitably coy when asked by MTV about his new record. 'I don't want to say too much about it,' he said. 'I want people to get what they get from it. It's definitely a new sound – not just from me, but period. I think it's cool. I hope everybody else does.'

More recently, pure-pop bands such as Steps experienced similar difficulties when going solo. This Pete Waterman-backed outfit was one of the UK's biggest live acts and sold millions of albums between 1997 and 2001, but their respective solo careers stalled almost before they had begun. Similarly, The Spice Girls ruled the world in the mid-1990s, but by the early 2000s, all the girls' solo careers had faltered and there was even speculation about a possible reunion tour.

There have been successes. Take That brought us Robbie Williams, of course, yet by contrast came the misfortune of Gary Barlow. The band's amiable singer-songwriter was widely touted as the new Elton John/George Michael, yet failed to establish a solo career of any repute. Likewise, Boyzone engendered Ronan Keating's strong-selling albums, but similar efforts by Mikey Graham and

'JUSTIN WANTS TO GO SOLO IN EVERY PART OF HIS LIFE'

The first chance the public got to find out in which direction Justin was heading came with his first solo single, 'Like I Love You', released in August 2002. An awesome opening gambit, the track was an immediate hit on radio and music television. Small wonder: this Neptunes-produced single was a perfectly crafted blend of Mexican acoustic guitars and down-and-dirty street hip-hop. An infectious dance tempo ensured that this track buried itself in the brain even after just one listen.

JT's vocal performance made this a standout track. The only weak point was the rather clumsy and affected spoken-word breaks by Justin. The same cannot be said for the rolling, funkily addictive rap break from Clipse, which cleverly bestowed street kudos to a performer who was, after all, still in the world's biggest boy band.

The video was superb, featuring model Shakara Ledard and some of the finest dance routines of recent times. Shot mostly outside a convenience store and in a nearby street, Justin's dancing was staggering. Detractors criticised him for aping Michael Jackson too much, but there was an undeniably new and refreshing veneer to his swift and complex moves. Musically, the single's most compulsive section was the quirky,

repetitive eight note close-out sequence, accompanied in the video by some amazing pseudo-robotic dancing from JT.

Interestingly, as a gauge of his immediate solo profile, Justin wore a 7-Eleven baseball cap in the video. That convenience store chain subsequently reported a massive run on the $8 caps, which had to be specially reordered to meet demand.

This odd fact was mirrored on a much larger scale by the song's commercial success. 'Like I Love You' entered the UK singles chart at number two, only held off the top spot by Nelly and Destiny's Child star Kelly Rowland's 'Dilemma'. It was also later nominated for a Grammy for 'Best Rap/Sung Collaboration'. Sales in the USA were also very strong and, more importantly perhaps, intrigued the record-buying public and music media about what else JT had up his sleeve.

If 'Like I Love You' had generated interest in Justin's solo album, the next single whipped curiosity into a frenzy. It is worth looking at this single in more depth, as it exemplifies why JT's solo work has been met with such acclaim and massive commercial success.

On its release, 'Cry Me A River' was an immediate global smash and the accompanying controversial video helped enormously in that. However, it was the song that was the star, in particular the arrangement and production.

On first listen, 'Cry Me A River' is a catchy, R&B-fused-with-hip-hop radio-friendly track which neatly continues the inventive and intriguing instrumentation already hinted at by the album's opening single, 'Like I Love You'. The lyrical slant talks of a relationship soured, a chance lost, a trust destroyed and the irrevocable damage that infidelity causes. But put 'Cry Me A River' on 'repeat', turn the stereo up loud and what unfolds is a modern pop classic.

The strength is in the production. The quantity of sounds, textures, genres and inflections in this near five-minute song is breathtaking. The intro alone is a mini-masterpiece. There is the rain-soaked sample seamlessly blended with a mock-operatic tenor, which then evolves within seconds into an almost Gregorian chant; this is effortlessly laid over a rising clarinet arpeggio and the song's central electronic trumpet-like riff; not satisfied with that, the final seconds of the intro, just before Justin's voice kicks in, brings forth a swell of four deep bursts of cello strings. Altogether a most peculiar concoction with which to start a song, but quite stunning nonetheless.

From thereon, 'Cry Me A River' gets much more complicated. The drumbeat of the song is essentially utterly simple: a plain double bass drum and tight snare. A traditional hand-clap effect lightens the pace but underpinning the entire song is a thrilling mixture of beatbox acrobatics, almost a hidden secret. This includes vocalised hi-hats, deep baritone notes, finger clicks and even near exasperated bursts that could almost be a guitar being picked or a pair of castanets. It all makes for a fabulous melting pot of human percussion. The effect is to somehow make this master class in ultra-modern production appear to come from around a burning, street corner brazier, with five or so hooded figures huddling nearby for warmth. Yet this is not a simple street

chant: it is one of the most complex pop songs of recent years.

Justin's lead vocals are simply staggering. At times taking the melody lead, then by contrast diving into the background to let the backing vocals rush to the fore, or alternatively using ultra-quick delivery and precisely clipped intonation to add his own beatbox to the maelstrom of sound. Stylishly, he leaves the chorus essentially simple, with the falsetto backing and softly spoken, regretful lyrics (the lyrics and melody were co-written by JT with Mosley and Storch).

The backing vocals stand alone as a separate instrument in their own right. At times, Justin's delivery is akin to a 1980s synth; elsewhere they are more like the orthodox, falsetto backing vocals usually reserved for female singers (although Justin is ably complemented by Timbaland, Marsha Ambroise, Tyrone Tribbet and Greater Anointing). Then the strings jump back in to mimic the backing vocals, jauntily thrusting the verse on, rejoining once again with a swirl as Justin heads into the next chorus.

Then there is the slow rap of the bridge, by Pharrell Williams: the deepest of deep ten-word one-liners, the final death sentence of a relationship that is terminally damaged. Both Pharrell and Justin arranged the vocals themselves, reportedly spending many dozens of hours perfecting the exact delivery.

As the song progresses, each one of these disparate elements dips in and out of the mix, which itself must have taken Jimmy Douglass and Timbaland hours and hours. Then, as the song rises to its climax, with all these intricately woven elements building to a crescendo, the track surprisingly breaks itself down, back to that street corner vocal group, yet somehow, at the same time, sounding for all the world like a church choir. The vocals mix Justin's loftiest falsetto with this choral backing and Pharrell's odd, effected vocal stabs, which distort into self-destruction and close the song on a suitably quirky note. It's such a complicated and intricate track that you could almost be forgiven for thinking this was the sound of the studio technology breaking up under the pressure.

In case this summary doesn't highlight all the skill that went into producing this classic song, just look at the liner notes produced by hip-hop legend Timbaland; there's an engineer for just the strings; a separate recording engineer; two mixers and an assistant engineer; hundreds of thousands of pounds worth of the most up-to-date studio technology . . . this is no ordinary pop song. But then JT is no ordinary pop star.

'Like I Love You' and 'Cry Me A River' perfectly teased the market for Justin's solo album, to be called *Justified*. Prior to the record's release in November 2002, Justin offered many hints at his influences and motivation for this, his first solo project: 'I wasn't consciously trying to make a non-'N Sync record,' he told Groovevolt.com. 'I was trying to make a multidimensional record, a record that captured the vibe of my favourite time in music, the 1960s. For the six weeks that we worked on these songs, I got to live in my own musical dream world and play a little hip-hop, a little old-school R&B, and a little classic rock. It was so much fun, and I learned a lot about making music in a totally different way than I'm used to.'

The album was recorded at Master Sound Studios in Virginia Beach and mixed at Windmark Recordings, also in that same town. The production partnerships on the album were bound to raise eyebrows – the duties were shared largely between the Neptunes and hip-hop kingpin Timbaland, who applied his trademark sound across much of the album. Pharrell Williams had met Justin in New York's Spa nightclub just prior to recording 'Girlfriend' with 'N Sync. They got on so well that a collaboration on the solo project was a must. These were some of the most highly respected voices in hip-hop and R&B.

Vocally, this record took JT to whole new areas, not least because R&B usually calls for a lower register and a more nasal tone. Yet, during the demanding recording sessions, Justin coped easily. As far back as his time in *The Mickey Mouse Club*, JT had been asked to sing R&B covers, as that show's producer Robin Wiley told *Vibe*, 'He had a lot of natural style and could sing anything you threw at him. I remember thinking, "Jeez, where did this kid come from?"' Likewise, as a child, Justin's favourite albums were by Stevie Wonder and Marvin Gaye, so this was not unfamiliar vocal territory.

Much of the album's energy comes from JT's insistence in the studio that they record as many elements as possible live. This spontaneous approach was then cleverly mixed with the aforementioned stellar production. However, Pharrell Williams denied that they were looking to overcomplicate the sound. 'If it's an apple, let it be an apple,' he said. 'We don't have to take a syringe and shoot some sugar into it.'

First up on *Justified* is the quirky opening track, 'Senorita'. Produced by the Neptunes' Pharrell Williams and Chad Hugo, as well as being co-written by that duo with JT, this track really sets the tone for the whole album. With Justin's spoken-word introduction, it is almost as if we have never heard of him before – and in a way, we haven't, at least not in this incarnation. The live vocals are mixed heavily up front, even leaving in Justin's question to the producer's booth, 'Come in right here?' Notably, Justin is introduced as a Memphis, Tennesse native, somehow validating the musical adventure that you are about to hear.

'Senorita' has a funky Latin feel, harmonised vocals and jaunty hand-clap rhythms. As if to confirm the chameleon-like metamorphosis JT

THE NEXT SINGLE WHIPPED CURIOSITY INTO A FRENZY

JUSTIFIED WAS A BRAVE, DIVERSE AND INCREDIBLE DEBUT ALBUM

achieves on this album, the guys-versus-ladies sing-off towards the end of the song is pulled off with panache, referenced by him as something they 'don't do anymore', an immediate insinuation that this record will be a blend of throwbacks and the ultra-modern. Quite remarkable really, had 'N Sync ever tried something as potentially crass as this, they would have crashed and burned without a doubt. The final 'good morning' to the ladies is a humorous jibe at Justin's own growing reputation as a Romeo.

With the next track, the hit single 'Like I Love You', the album enjoys its first classic song. It successfully ups the ante for the album but, fortunately, is not a pearl among swine. This single is ably followed by the Eastern-sounding and mysterious, yet saucy, '(Oh No) What You Got'. Timbaland's vast production experience is vital to this song, where he somehow successfully mixes Arabian flutes with a 1980s synth arpeggio and another deft rap from Clipse. As with the previous track, the vocals are arranged by JT and Pharrell, with a complex multilayered mix of rap, backing vocals, pop melodies and skittering R&B. In a vein that runs throughout the record, the production pulls back towards the close of the song, revealing Justin's vocals as the main instrument, while the Pro Tools programming and sophisticated production takes a restrained back seat. There is a whiff of early Janet Jackson to the whole song, although this was not a track she actually worked on. Easily a great single should he choose to release it, '(Oh No) What You Got' comfortably matches the standard set by 'Like I Love You'.

Next up is the rather weak ballad, 'Take It From Here'. After three such funky slices of JT's own take on pop/hip-hop/R&B, it is disappointing to revert to type and record a gentle ballad that could easily have come straight from the recording sessions for a new 'N Sync album. The usual attributes were there and it was polished enough. At times Justin's vocals sound more like Green from Scritti Politti than the more often cited influences. The jaunty strings came courtesy of Charles Veal and the Southwest Chamber Orchestra, rather than a computer programme, but this still didn't lift the song out of its sugary foundations. A necessity perhaps, but not a highlight.

The main problem with the above track is that it precedes the album's best song, the afore-mentioned 'Cry Me A River'. The difficulty when you have written a song such as this is where to put it on the album. Too soon and the remainder of the record seems poor by comparison; too late and it feels wasted. Justin was aware of this problem with 'Cry Me A River' so he plumped right for the centre of the record. By now, the listener was certain that when Pharrell Williams said to Justin that 'your album is a very serious record, brother,' he was not joking.

Future single 'Rock Your Body' takes up the gauntlet laid down by 'Cry Me A River' with aplomb. Again, the use of super-funky guitar flicks gives this track an instant retro feel – an almost mutated disco hybrid. Once more Justin uses his high vocals to clever effect, mixing them here with semi-rap, melodic scats on the bridges. The high-in-the-mix bass line is pure thumping funk, particularly during the bass and vocal break, while the sassy female backing vocals,

courtesy of Vanessa Marquez, lift the song up another notch. The hand claps are in full force again, reminding the listener of an era that finished well before Justin was even born. More beatbox acrobatics elaborate the otherwise fairly basic instrumentation of the song towards the climax, surely a direct antecedent of the same techniques used on 'N Sync's hit single 'Pop'. More Michael Jackson/Stevie Wonder comparisons abound of course, but here it is more referential than derivative.

The peculiar but strangely addictive 'Nothin' Else' is up next. Justin provides his own Jackson backing vocals, while the lead verse line is deeper, controlled and altogether more odd. A simple backdrop keeps the song's lines clean, but then it winds up perfectly into the disco-style chorus, with a pop melody at its most intense. It reminds the listener of both classic 1970s-era disco while at the same time sounding exactly like a cast-off from a session by French dance-meisters Air. Sure, this track could also have been on *Off The Wall* – the vocal bridge needs re-examining time after time to make sure it isn't actually the King of Pop making a cameo appearance – but, sitting here as it did among a post-Millennial mix of funk, hip-hop, R&B and pure pop, it

seemed a natural fit. Final confirmation too that Justin Timberlake is a Stevie Wonder fanatic.

Britney fans/haters were intrigued by the next 'break-up' song, 'Last Night'. Synth-laden and chock-full of percussive detail, the song was yet another sophisticated production courtesy of the Neptunes. With songs like this, it was easy to see why Justin would soon be enjoying a huge following in the urban music world. Listen in particular to the way the lush string arrangements sit beautifully side by side with a rhythm section straight out of a Snoop Dogg gangsta rap number and a vocal line that dips equally into the best bits of 1970s and 1980s dance. Janet Jackson's 'Together Again' must have been on Justin's CD player when he recorded this track.

Disappointingly, it is back to the saccharine ballads next, the near Michael Jackson tribute/parody, 'Still On My Brain'. Most obviously a nod to the latter's 'You Are Not Alone', the song is just too derivative, too bluntly a reference to the past. Justin's strength is his ability to mix past, present and future in a unique and compelling way, but here the record falls off track. From a callously commercial point of view, however, tracks such as this and 'Take It From Here' kept his profile high within the older female market, yet another corner of the music-buying public that he seemed able to win over.

Throughout the album, there are countless lyrics that could be interpreted as references to Britney Spears and this song is a case in point. That said, it was also a generic love song in the main, so it was easy for JT to sidestep such questions. The brilliance of the instrumentation, production and delivery of these lyrics almost made the actual meaning of the words secondary.

Thrusting the listener straight back on to the street corner is the next track, the slinky, bass-heavy '(And She Said) Take Me Now', with its additional vocals by Janet Jackson. Brilliant, seedy and eerie raps from Timbaland add to the spooky sound. Again, the battling lead, backing and rap vocals compete with one another without

pushes the song towards its close. As with other tracks on the album, Justin was really mixing with the musical elite.

Next we come to the penultimate track, 'Let's Take A Ride'. The 1980s-style vocal intro sets a summery scene and you can almost imagine JT cruising to this tune in his Mercedes supercar. One of the few excursions into vocal narrative, JT is taking his belle out in his wheels to forget her troubles, one of which is losing her job. A straight-ahead dance track, clean and simple.

Finally, we have the sugary Brian McKnight-produced ballad, 'Never Again'. You could almost be forgiven for thinking you had dreamed JT's solo career and this was in fact the new 'N Sync album. This sentimental song, with its possible references to Ms Spears again, is perhaps an

JUSTIN WAS REALLY MIXING
WITH THE MUSICAL ELITE

ever cluttering the mix. Stylistically, Timbaland and co-producer Scott Storch somehow fuse together elements of disco, pure 1980s funk and dub.

Once more the musical backdrop could easily be spliced on to a hardcore rap chart hit, but here JT chooses to stick with his funky leanings. Arguably one of his finest vocal moments on the album, this is one of five songs he was solely responsible for vocally arranging (and the remaining eight he co-arranged, mostly with Pharrell Williams).

The quirky flavours are continued with the infectious 'Right For Me', the album's funkiest single track. This time Justin vocally swerves towards *Purple Rain*-era Prince, intriguingly accompanied by yet more beatbox sounds and hand claps. Breathtaking percussion exudes from this track, courtesy of the world-leading specialists Vidal Davis and Frank 'Knuckles' Walker. The fabulous guest rap from Bubba Sparxxx brilliantly

excessively soft close to the album. It is difficult not to be slightly disappointing that the record doesn't finish with a harder R&B gesture, but this is still a polished and rich sound.

Justified was a brave, diverse and incredible debut album. Agreed, it had its weak moments, and certainly there were very clear signs of where Justin had got some of his inspiration and influences from. But the whole package was so well produced, so deftly woven together and so addictively flavoured that it was hard not to see this record as anything other than a triumph. The question was, would the public at large and the hard-to-please music press agree?

The signs were not necessarily good that Justin would please the critics. On the release of 'Like I Love You', he had performed at the MTV Video Music Awards in the USA, watched by an audience of tens of millions. His performance – complete with fedora hat, glove and moonwalk (although wisely no crotch-grab) – brought him scathing reviews from many critics, who pilloried him for simply copying Michael Jackson, rather than being influenced by him. Justin's performance provoked this comment from Jim Farber of the *New York Daily News*: 'Timberlake won the "Most Flagrant Michael Jackson Impersonation" . . . he didn't even imitate a classic.' When these same critics saw the video for 'Like I Love You', with Justin's Jacko-style dance routines, falsetto vocal yelps, heavy breathing and again similar garb, these criticisms were reinforced. Maybe, with the benefit of hindsight, Justin's choice of performance style was just a little too blatant. After all, Jacko's greatest live moment arguably came when he performed the moonwalk at the Grammy Awards in 1983. This negative reaction at the MTV awards ceremony was a bitterly disappointing start for Justin but not one that would hold him down for long.

JT makes no secret of his reverence for Michael Jackson. Indeed, the two stars have become close friends. When the latter was the subject of furore over a documentary made by British journalist Martin Bashir – which Jackson later declared a complete 'betrayal' – many people actually felt sorry for the King of Pop. Justin was one of them and was surprisingly furious about the matter. At the Brit Awards in February 2003, he asked organisers to make sure he did not bump into Bashir. 'That guy is despicable. He had better keep out of my way.' Justin was angry, but others were far more disgusted – Bashir received death threats before the ceremony and opted to stay away.

Justin did not try to deny Jackson's influence, as he told Z100 Radio: 'I think this whole generation is influenced by Michael, I think Michael has influenced Britney, I think Michael has influenced Nelly. I would be a fool to say that Michael has not influenced me. I used to run around when I was like four or five years old with a big afro wig on singing "ABC . . . easy as 123". You know I thought I was Michael.' He even said he was flattered by the comparisons. Justin's own collaborators also highlighted the connection. Timbaland said, 'Justin's album is too crazy. The stuff I did for him is Michael Jackson all over again.' For those who felt Justin was too young to be compared to the living legend, it is worth noting that Michael released *Off The Wall* when he was also 21.

Justin did not try to hide the fact that Jackson's *Off The Wall* album was an inspiration for the recording of *Justified*. Furthermore, JT's producer, Pharrell Williams, told *Vibe* magazine how he dusted off five songs he'd put forward – but which had been rejected – for Jackson's *HIStory Volume 1* album. These songs were comprehensively reworked and rewritten to create new tracks, namely, 'Senorita', 'Let's Take A Ride', 'Last Night', 'Nothin' Else' and 'Take It From Here'.

Justin's style was similar to Michael's in many ways too, the familiar fedora hat and glove being the most obvious connection. However, Justin had evolved his own style that was quite distinct. He often wore long-sleeved shirts under T-shirts, hooded tops under leather jackets and more casual gear than Jackson was usually seen in. Justin did share a passion for

the extravagant – a huge diamond stud in each ear and an encrusted $100,000 watch being just two dazzling examples.

Also, due to his work with Wade Robson, a former Jackson and Prince choreographer, Justin's dance moves clearly shared some genetic common ground with Jackson's. Just looking at the video for 'Like I Love You' alone confirms this. (Interestingly, R&B veteran Usher is said to take great exception to being usurped in the eyes of the media as pop's greatest mover.)

However, for the generation of fans buying Justin's music, and indeed for those that had bought so any of Michael's records, the comparison was undermined by one startling fact: Michael Jackson had not released a 'classic' album for many years. His dwindling record sales were not helped by a very difficult relationship with the press and, most damagingly of all, the allegations made against him concerning alleged child abuse (which were subsequently subject to an out of court settlement). The result of all this was that the 'Wacko Jacko' persona threatened to engulf Jackson to such an extent that the genius behind such songs as 'Billie Jean' and the *Thriller* album seemed almost from another life.

Whatever the similarities to Jackson, one point is clear: each new generation wants its own icons, its own stars. Teenage pop-punk fans want Blink 182, not the Buzzcocks; younger Usher fans don't want to listen to New Edition; teenage Foo Fighter fanatics have little interest in Black Sabbath.

Jacko's watershed *Thriller* album may indeed still hold the record as the best-selling album ever at over 40 million copies, but that was

in 1983, when Justin was two. So many Justin Timberlake fans are younger than the star himself, and were therefore not even born in Jackson's heyday. Many will see *Thriller* and *Off The Wall* as records their parents listen too (like Justin's mum, Lynn, who would have been just 23).

Just as songs are endlessly covered and remixed, so artists necessarily have to look to stars of the past in order to create something fresh for the present and the future. Sixteen-year-old JT fans want Justin, not Michael Jackson. The fact is, *Justified* was the album Michael Jackson should have made instead of 2001's *Invincible*.

With industry observers crowning Justin as the pop world's greatest dancer – an accolade previously the exclusive domain of Jacko – it appeared distinctly possible that future records by Michael would perhaps be held up in comparison to Justin Timberlake's. By April 2003, style bible *The Face* had even put JT on their front cover, suggesting he was the artist for the new Millennium. Their banner headline: 'The King of Pop'.

CHAPTER 5:
THE LIFESTYLES O
FAMOUS

THE RICH AND

Compared with the record-breaking sales of 'N Sync's previous two albums, initial figures for *Justified* seemed quite muted. In America, the record sold less than half a million copies, almost a fifth of the sales of *No Strings Attached*. This meant *Justified* entered the Billboard charts at number two, kept off the top slot by the all-conquering Eminem, whose excellent soundtrack to his acclaimed debut film *8 Mile* sold 60,000 more records than Justin that week. In the UK, the album went into the top ten and appeared capable of remaining there, but figures were again only modestly good. This was a similar tale around the globe. A good start, but not a staggering one.

Fortunately, *Justified* was met with a very strong critical response, a facet that 'N Sync

'has the potential to have an impact similar to Mary J Blige's classic *What's the 411?* or D'Angelo's groundbreaking *Brown Sugar*.' High praise indeed.

The *Daily News* said, 'In most tracks, springy beats and original sound effects give the songs surprising texture and distinction,' while *Rolling Stone* wished to highlight the role of the producers: 'The Neptunes' brilliant, impertinent, full-body funk is, for the most part, what stays with you from *Justified*; their songs, spacious and shot through with ecstatic aaahs, outshine their neighbours on the album.'

NME looked at the record from a loftier angle. In an otherwise uncharitable review, they did admit that, 'this is, culturally, a significant album. Not because of the music but because it's the first concerted attempt by a white teen artist

JUSTIN HAS BEEN BORN WITH A SENSE OF HUMOUR

struggled to achieve and one which, in this particular instance, was to play a vital part in the accelerating sales of Justin's album and its eventual longevity in charts around the world. Take this snippet from *The Observer*: 'Inventive and instant, grindingly raw and sexy, it's a truly great record.' Notably, the expected positivity in the pop and mainstream press was complemented by an unexpected rash of strong reviews in the urban, hip-hop and R&B press. *Vibe* magazine gave JT an unexpected front cover feature, unusual for a white artist, saying the album,

to cross over to a black audience since George Michael. It's a sign of the times – an indication that teen pop in America is dead on its feet and that the "urban" (i.e. black) audience is running the Billboard Hot 100.'

Of course, some critics were quick to exaggerate this premise and slight Justin by saying he was simply plundering R&B and soul for his own ends. 'If *Justified* wasn't a Timberlake release, there would be no hype because it's simply another CD full of average material,' said Eric Danton of the *Hartford Courant*. 'The production

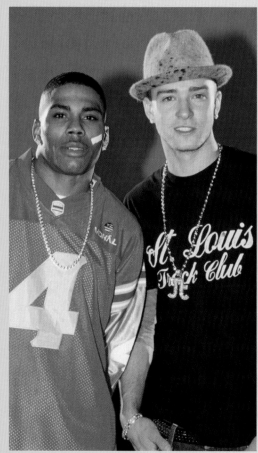

is stellar, if slick . . . but not even guest spots from Janet Jackson, Bubba Sparxxx and Brian McKnight can make the songs compelling.' *Justified* did receive its fair share of critical indifference with many people saying he was leaning too much on the credibility of his collaborators. In reply, Justin would just have to prove his detractors wrong and make the record a smash.

Aside from the aforementioned brilliance of the album and Justin's developing ultra-cool persona, there were other factors behind *Justified*'s ability to progress rapidly from this only above-average start to become one of the biggest-selling albums of the last few years. For one, unlike so many celebrities, Justin has been born with a sense of humour, which was particularly well received in the UK. His first TV appearance

in support of the solo album in Britain was on *Johnny Vaughan Tonight*, where Justin was disarmingly self-deprecating and happily joined in the fooling around with puddings and grand-mothers. On a similar US TV show called *All That*, which starred Britney's sister, Jamie Lynn Spears, he took a barrage of insults and even allowed his one-time potential sister-in-law to drop his trousers and then sloppily kiss him (albeit dressed as an 80-year-old bodyguard).

Justin has also captured a strong gay following. He started the ball rolling with a homoerotic photo shoot, all bloody-nosed and stripped, in *Arena Hommes Plus* (the photographer, Stephen Klein, later took the album shots for JT's solo record), and is rumoured to be considering a one-off role as a gay hairdresser in the smash sitcom *Friends*. He was also spotted dancing with

Britney at a gay nightclub and mentioned that he would be interested in a part in the film version of *Rent*.

Like 'N Sync before him, Justin enjoyed much reflected kudos by his canny choice of collaborators. The album's producers – Timbaland and the Neptunes – were an obvious case in point, but Justin also released a single with the rap star of the moment, Nelly, in February 2003. 'Work It' helped to raise JT's cool-factor another notch. The high-vocal rapping style of Nelly had made him a revelation in the sometimes repetitive world of mainstream hip-hop, and his album *Welcome To Nellyville* was a multiplatinum, award-winning global smash. Nelly did JT's prospective solo credibility no harm when he spoke highly of his colleague, saying rather obtusely, 'He's a cool dirty. Once I found out he was from Memphis, that sewed it up for me. I was like, "OK, I see you in a whole new light. You Memphis family."'

In the hilarious and near X-rated video for 'Work It', Nelly and Justin star as gardeners at Hugh Hefner's *Playboy* mansion. While Hefner is absent, the scheming duo dress in the *Playboy* owner's trademark smoking jackets and cavort around the grounds with increasingly scantily clad ladies. It is a hard life, but someone has to do it.

All of the above generously helped sustain interest in *Justified*. However, there was one single factor that made the popularity of the album explode exponentially: the video for second single, 'Cry Me A River'. Directed by maverick Francis Lawrence, this promo clip was a superb, if not a little disturbing, psychodrama. Set in the home Justin is sharing with his 'fictitious' philandering partner, there is an edge of surrealism to the plush, minimalist pop star mansion, not least from the fact that Justin flies around the rooms and levitates precariously from worktops and ledges. As his rapping sidekick waits outside, Justin calls in a mystery brunette, who strips off and then videos their amorous activity. It is left unclear as to whether she is earning her living or is a friend, but the dismissive nod she gets

JT WAS FINALLY GETTING THE LONGEVITY AND SOLO SUCCESS HE SO CRAVED

when it is time for her to run through the pouring rain and enter the house for her pre-arranged liaison, leaves an undeniable scent of seediness.

Then the video twists: a blonde Britney lookalike arrives in a Porsche 911. She parks up and enters the house, believing it to be empty. Justin stalks her round the house, even disconcertingly sniffing her hair. As she showers, Justin watches her, waiting for her to enter the bedroom and discover the videotape of his recent infidelity replayed and then paused in all its glory. Revenge is had.

With the powerful combination of a swanky setting, peculiar special effects and the obvious Britney–Justin intrigue, the video was immediately in massive demand from music television channels around the globe, ensuring the single was an international smash. Despite claiming it was just 'the director having fun', the obvious insinuations about Britney are hard to ignore. Ms Spears wears a similar trademark hat to the blonde in the video, drives a Porsche, wears similar sunglasses, sports a tattoo of a fairy on her back, like the porcelain one Justin props the door open with, and is strikingly similar looking to the blonde woman taking a shower in the video. Nevertheless, Justin was insistent this was not a direct slight on his ex, saying, 'When you watch it, either you have a sense of humour or you don't. The girl doesn't represent anybody. I haven't gone public about my relationship.'

Yet, confusingly, he admits to phoning Britney before the video was released to the media, in order to pre-empt any 'misunderstanding', which is in itself an implicit admission that there is a clear undercurrent. As a result of this controversial footage, this single and the famous video were a real shot in the arm for the sales of *Justified*. Album sales started to pick up momentum and Justin's PR office was besieged with calls for interviews. It appeared that JT was finally getting the longevity and solo success he so craved.

With the campaign for *Justified* finally gathering speed, Justin was dealt a painful and inconvenient blow when he broke his foot in November 2002, while rehearsing for several upcoming television appearances, and was forced to reluctantly cancel a series of forthcoming Canadian appearances, as well as dates in the UK and France.

Nevertheless, the momentum just kept gathering, such that in January 2003, *Justified* finally climbed to the top of the UK album charts, ahead of a lengthy spell in the top ten. This feat

JUSTIN WASTED NO TIME IN ENJOYING HIS NEW BACHELOR STATUS

was mirrored across Europe and in his native USA, where sales were snowballing. Justin Timberlake, the solo star, had arrived.

The public's growing fascination with Justin went much further than just his music. Although he was no longer with Britney, questions about their relationship still flooded in and, eventually, Justin gave out a little more detail than perhaps he might have originally planned. When she opened her restaurant, NYLA, he didn't show up and, worse still, rain-soaked fans were kept chanting 'Justin! Justin!' When JT then appeared on the Barbra Walters chat show, he sang a track called 'Horrible Woman', which made reference to a dumped lover running crying back to her mother, an ex who he cruelly described as not even worth the gas in his BMW. It was hard not to suspect this was Britney, although JT hastily pointed out that the song was actually written over two years previously, when the celebrity couple were still a happy item. However, this song and his other more tabloid comments led to accusations that JT was using his former relationship with Britney to reignite his initially slow-burning album campaign. Although both parties insisted

there was no animosity, it perhaps came as no surprise when lyrics to an unreleased Britney song, 'Clubsong', which detailed a former lover's angry thoughts of verbal revenge, were unearthed by the media.

Having finally split from Britney some time around April 2002, Justin wasted no time in enjoying his new bachelor status. Remember, for years, while Britney had been proud to declare she would not sleep with her man until they were married, poor old Justin was left in the unenviable position of being the man who was with a sex symbol but couldn't actually have sex with her. Cue thousands of bar-room jokes at his expense.

Justin was barely into his twenties, had had one serious relationship for much of his young life, was wealthy beyond imagination, good-looking and super-famous. Naturally, it didn't take long for reports of amorous activity to filter through to an all too eager tabloid media. At one early stage, they cruelly hyped a (non-existent) relationship with Lance Bass's ex, Daniele Fishel. Other columnists briefly mentioned include Liam Gallagher's future wife, Nicole Appleton, as well as Destiny's Child's Beyoncé Knowles.

However, Justin was clearly not about to settle down again too quickly. Next, he was rumoured to be dating the beautiful Janet Jackson. They had met before at numerous music industry events, as well as during 'N Sync's support slots on the aforementioned *Velvet Rope* tour.

Janet herself was a fine example of a pure-pop starlet who had evolved over time into an R&B icon. Her career progression had several marked similarities to the task now facing Justin with his first solo record. Like Justin, Janet enjoyed more early success for her TV roles, most notably in *Good Times*, *Diff'rent Strokes* and *Fame*. Her eponymous album did solid business but it was her third album, 1986's *Control*, which catapulted her into superstardom. Janet's early records succeeded in moving her out of the shadow of her brother and the Jackson family, with multiplatinum success across the world. However, it was *Velvet Rope* that changed her public persona so dramatically, including widespread approval of her choice of big-name collaborators.

When Ms Jackson worked on the sessions for *Justified*, it became apparent that she and Justin were much more than just good friends. Thus it was clear that working with Janet was not just an exciting musical venture for Justin. She had

already lived through a career that carried so many parallels to his own, and this swathe of common ground meant the two became very close very quickly. Some tabloids even went so far as to suggest that Janet had asked Justin to father her baby (denied by both parties). The couple fuelled the gossip when they were seen kissing at Missy Elliott's birthday party in July 2002.

Justin kept his usual cool head when plagued with questions about his closeness to Janet. 'Did Janet want me for my body? You should ask her. I don't know. Did you ever consider it was vice versa?' Whatever the truth, Justin clearly has a lot of affection for Janet, telling her via his album sleeve notes that, 'You are a beautiful person inside and out. I can't wait to work with you again. Thank you for being my friend.'

With the Janet rumours suitably evaded, Justin was back in the romantic spotlight soon after. Next up was a fling with US television actress Alyssa Milano, star of the oddly sexy sci-fi show *Charmed*. Some ten years his senior, Alyssa met Justin in a fashionable Los Angeles bar. Much to the tabloids' delight, she visited Justin on the set of the video shoot for 'Like I Love You' and, according to *People* magazine, 'the pair spent the better part of the day in Timberlake's trailer.' By December 2002, however, they were finished and she was rumoured to be stepping out with Limp Bizkit's Fred Durst, who would shortly also be seen dating . . . Britney Spears.

Around the same time, Justin was questioned over his closeness to an 'N Sync backing dancer called Jenna Dewan. They went to the 2002 Grammy Awards as a couple and were seen openly raunchily dancing with each other. When Justin later bought her a BMW, tongues inevitably started to wag and it was widely believed they dated for a while. The problem was, the new German auto arrived on Jenna's drive at the same time that Justin was supposedly still dating Alyssa. Rumours that Dewan and JT were getting married only exacerbated the confusion.

Justin worked with famed diva Mariah Carey on her album *Charm Bracelet* and whispers quickly

IT WAS CLEAR THAT WORKING WITH JANET WAS NOT JUST AN EXCITING MUSICAL VENTURE FOR JUSTIN

circulated that their studio work was not the extent of their liaison, again denied by both parties. Similarly, new R&B star Alicia Keys was seen enjoying an intimate lunch with JT, which even stretched as far as kissing. She later claimed that their friendship was not sexual at all and had centred around writing music together.

The one alleged sortée Justin had which must have really appalled his former belle Britney Spears was with a newly defrocked Christina Aguilera. As mentioned, the trio had all worked together since their pre-teen days on *The Mickey Mouse Club*. Once both Christina and Britney started having hits, talk of a bitter rivalry quickly developed, the general consensus being that Britney was sexier, more amenable and more successful.

Christina is the subject of many 'diva' allegations, with stories of tantrums, backstage demands and generally outrageous pop star egotistical behaviour. More shocking perhaps was the transformation she underwent for the launch of her latest album in 2002. Gone were the twee outfits and sugary pop of her former releases. In their place was a fashion sense that seemed straight off the red-lit street corner, including an infamous pair of leather chaps, worn over

only black knickers and with the legend 'Dirty' emblazoned on the back of the belt. The near X-rated video for her number one smash single 'Dirty' caused outrage, particularly when she performed the same sizzling hot dance routines on several children's TV shows. Ridiculed by many for her peculiar fashion sense, Christina seemed at pains to wear as little as possible. The accompanying bestselling album was modestly titled *Stripped*.

Justin, a 22-year-old man just coming out of his first long-term relationship of four years, was rumoured to have reacted the way most men of that age would to a scantily clad, curvaceous blonde pop star who made no secret of the fact she was interested in him: he reciprocated (allegedly). Despite rumours he was anxious to meet a girl who had as much brains as curves, Justin's considered opinion on the shocking new Christina was, 'She's looking kind of hot these days.' Again, there was no authority to corroborate these whispers.

The celebrity duo were seen at many parties together and the inevitable 'canoodling' was also reported, but there seems little evidence that the two have ever been a serious item. One fact is certain – they are going to work together in the

future. By the New Year of 2003, the pair were reported to be planning a summer co-headlining tour together, namely the *Justified and Stripped* tour.

Some insiders close to JT said he had even started dating a local girl who lived near his house, who was not a celebrity at all. To cloud the picture still further, February 2003 saw rumours that Justin and Britney were together again, even going so far as to describe a passionate night at her New York apartment and off-the-record quotes from Justin saying he was still in love with Britney. He was obviously still emotionally raw from their break-up and often in interviews would not refer to her by name. He told *Rolling Stone*, 'I think I still have a lot of feelings, though I don't particularly know what they are . . . I may not ever get over her. But I still love her, I really do still love that girl.' How these sorts of statements will resound in light of his very public dalliances with the above melee of women remains to be seen.

The problem was, although JT said the occasional warm words for Ms Spears, his public behaviour suggested he was having the time of his life. Justin's Midas touch at this time contrasted sharply with the apparent misfortunes of Britney. She was experiencing difficult times, with reports

of chain-smoking, swearing and generally more rock-and-roll antics. After the release of her global smash debut, 'Hit Me Baby (One More Time)', the teenage Britney could do no wrong for the first four years of her career. However, by 2002, this formula looked to be running out of steam.

Like Christina, Britney seemed desperate to throw off the shackles of her squeaky-clean image. At the London premiere of her debut feature film, the critically panned but commercially successful *Crossroads*, Britney angered the huge crowd of fans, who had waited for hours to cheer their heroine, by simply getting out of her limo, walking into the cinema and offering a brief, cursory wave as she disappeared into the building. TV reports the next morning showed pre-teen fans sobbing and mothers angrily recounting how much time and money their daughters had spent on the seemingly ungrateful Ms Spears.

Britney eventually gave up trying to pretend she never drank or smoked at all. At one showbiz event, she turned up wearing a T-shirt bearing the slogan, 'F*** You!' Soon after, she started dating Fred Durst, front man for hard nu-metal rockers Limp Bizkit. Although this affair soon crumbled amid suggestions that Fred found Britney too high maintenance, the blonde, good Christian

'I STILL LOVE HER, I REALLY DO STILL LOVE THAT GIRL'

southern gal, whose favourite phrase had formerly been 'Oh, my gosh!', had clearly turned a corner into an altogether more downbeat street. The fact that this coincided with her split from Justin and decidedly muted sales for her almost self-referential and rather repetitive third album supported suggestions that Ms Spears might be facing tough times ahead. Matters did not improve with the leak of a confidential document from within the Britney camp that detailed the obstacles in her path and highlighted 'the Justin issue' as a major debilitating factor.

Furthermore, while snaps of Britney ranged from strained to downright glum, Justin was pictured having the time of his life. As Ms Spears paraded her latest beau, bad boy actor Colin Farrell at the latter's Hollywood premiere for his film *The Recruit*, Justin was dressing up as a dolphin for a surprise cameo appearance on *Top of the Pops*. While the hugely credible Flaming Lips performed their hit 'Yoshimi Battles The Pink Robots Pt 1', the camera struggled to focus on the six-foot two-inch tall, blue, furry dolphin playing bass. While a six-foot rabbit played keyboards (the Lips are famed for this sartorially bestial kink on stage), Justin whipped off the dolphin mask and continued to play the actual

bass line for the remainder of the song, with a huge beaming smile across his face. This odd collaboration was the result of Lips front man Wayne Coyne and Justin meeting at BBC Radio 1 and exchanging compliments about each other. Hardly the actions of a broken-hearted man!

While Justin is seen by many as a top international playboy and pop star lothario, he has in fact had his heart broken no less than three times. When he was only fifteen, his girlfriend cheated on him and he was distraught, breaking up with her immediately after. Then, as 'N Sync took off, he struggled to keep a relationship going over eighteen months only to see that girlfriend also eventually cheat on him. Then there was Britney, whose infidelity Justin preferred to play down, instead describing how they had lost the trust between them. Justin is therefore an odd mix – one of the world's most eligible bachelors yet ultimately, to date, a loser in love. 'They've all gone down the same way. Three strikes, I'm out.'

CHAPTER 6:
NO MORE THE MUM

MY'S BOY

WHEN IT WAS ANNOUNCED THAT JUSTIN AND KYLIE WOULD BE PERFORMING A DUET, THE TONGUES WERE WAGGING INSTANTLY

It wasn't just Britney Spears who was on the wrong end of some negative press during this time. Justin was the subject of several critical reports saying he was becoming an egotistical superstar. One example was when he ate at London's Planet Hollywood restaurant and was alleged to have shushed away young fans asking for an autograph, as well as taking over an entire corner of the room with a gaggle of burly and intimidating bodyguards – all at lunchtime on a weekday when no one was really bothering him. Other reports of him refusing to sign autographs and being rude to fans also began to circulate.

Justin defended himself by saying in USA Today; 'We're young guys, and we like to have fun, and we make mistakes sometimes. We don't say that we lead squeaky-clean lives. But we were raised by good mothers and good families, and we always take them into consideration.'

It seems that Justin is true to his word regarding his beloved mother. His close relationship with Lynn Harless has even been cited by himself as a reason why so many potential girlfriends fall short. 'You keep looking for someone as good as your mother, and that's a losing battle.'

Justin says his private side is best known by his mother and also admits that when he comes off tour and needs to wind down, he returns home to the family dogs, Bearlie and Bella, while his mum knows exactly what to cook for him and how to look after him. Pass the saucepan, Christina?

The Timberlake family home is a mixture of a mother's shrine to her famous son and an arcade of pop star extravagance. Full-size pinball machines stand next to massive hi-tech plasma TV screens, on which Justin plays the latest video games. Yet, everywhere there are pictures of Lynn's baby boy, which he has been known to turn face down when she is out of the room.

Lynn is often seen out on the town with Justin. She wears Harley Davidson T-shirts, smokes Virginia Slims and, more often than not, retires for the night long after her pop star son does! His adoration of his mother was captured in ink in 2002 when JT had a 'guardian angel' motif with his mother's initials in gothic script tattooed between his shoulder blades.

Quite where potential partners like Christina Aguilera and Justin's mother meet in some kind of perfect hybrid of a girlfriend is not clear. Justin explains; 'I want a girl who I can tell anything to and not worry about offending them. I've always been that way with my mother. We really converse well.' Meanwhile, his mum says occasionally Justin will divulge a little too much graphic detail of his sexual exploits when asking her for advice. This is one of the rare times when she will suggest he confides instead in his childhood best friend, Trace Ayala. Perhaps this is where Christina might start to fit the bill as a girlfriend. After all, Christina once sheepishly sang, 'I need that, uh, to get me off, sweat until my clothes come off.'

The rumours about his relationship with Christina Aguilera were just about fading when the pair were spotted at the super-trendy Sketch restaurant doing what tabloid paparazzi love best – 'canoodling' again. The A-list crowd was celebrating London Fashion Week, after which an invited few retired to The Ten Room Club, reserved for those extra-special people. Here, Justin sang an hour-long set with N.E.R.D., while a gaggle of top celebs watched, including Janet Jackson, Kylie Minogue, Jade Jagger and model Catalina. Janet stood just a few yards from Christina, both of them hollering and dancing along to the music. A fabled tabloid 'insider' told *The Sun* that, 'Christina wanted Justin to herself and was impatient when he wouldn't get off the stage.' When he finally did, they disappeared into the VIP area (of this VIP club) for the remainder of the night. Unconfirmed reports suggested the pair retired to his hotel later that night.

Thus far, Justin's alleged affairs had made him a staple of the tabloid gossip columns. However, his next famous flirtation – with the vertically challenged Princess of Pop, antipodean Kylie Minogue – would take him on to the front

pages of all the UK's tabloids. Justin's peerless ability to manipulate/massage the press for maximum effect is perfectly displayed by this rumoured sortée with Ms Minogue. The former child star and *Neighbours* legend had experienced a first flush of chart success way back in the late 1980s, enjoying nineteen top forty hits (including four chart-toppers and nine top five hits) produced by the then omnipresent Stock, Aitken and Waterman pop factory. After the hits ran dry, Kylie tried to make several comebacks, most credibly with a polished but commercially unsuccessful album for the revered Deconstruction label, which was also met with tepid critical interest.

However, one song changed everything: the single 'Can't Get You Out Of My Head' had been a colossal comeback smash. The song, a modern pop classic, had shifted in excess of one million copies in the UK alone, making it the fortieth bestselling single ever in that country. In the process, Kylie was relaunched as a pop queen for the new Millennium. Re-signed to EMI, Kylie had already released three singles prior to this (including the number one 'Spinning Around') but it was this particular track that cemented her place in the pop pantheon. It also won its writers – one of whom was former pop star Cathy Dennis – a prestigious Ivor Novello songwriting award. Kylie's corresponding album, *Fever*, met with massive multiplatinum success and a string of sold-out international dates.

More bizarrely, the media became fixated with Kylie's buttocks. Although J-Lo was the undefeated champion of the prize butt, Kylie was a serious contender. As her mini-skirts got

increasingly smaller, to the point where they vanished altogether and turned into a lingerie brand (the self-effacingly named Love Kylie), the public were bombarded with close-ups of the famous Minogue tush. The more the rear was featured, the more the newspapers sold. At one point, the rumour mill even suggested she had had plastic surgery on the cheeks (angrily denied), both of which were declared a national obsession. The hysteria surrounding Kylie's bum reached a peak when Madame Tussaud's unveiled a waxwork of the pop star in a barely dignified on-all-fours position, her rearmost uppermost.

Thus we came to the Brit Awards 2003, at Earl's Court, west London. Justin was asked by the Brit Award organisers to choose a female duet partner for the night. Having met Kylie at a New York TV show called *The Jingle Ball* he made

no hesitation in singling her out. Purportedly Justin phoned Kylie himself to ask her. When it was announced that Justin and Kylie would be performing a duet, the tongues were wagging instantly. On the actual night, however, no one could have imagined the furore that was about to explode.

It is fair to say that Kylie is not afraid to flaunt her body, on this occasion relying on that old faithful, the barely there mini-skirt. Those up close to the stage may also have caught sight (if they were looking that high up) of specially commissioned jewellery that Kylie was wearing, a necklace and bracelet made by Johnny Rocket, both bearing the initials 'JT'. As Kylie and Justin gyrated to an altogether intriguing version of Blondie's 'Rapture', Justin seized his moment and his, er, pound of flesh. He slapped his palm

soundly on pop's royal posterior – the dreams of a million men in his hands, framed perfectly by his puckered lips and ecstatic facial expression. Quite deliberate, quite calculated and quite brilliant in its impact.

The following day, despite the impending war with Iraq, all the talk was of this 'historic' moment. To add to the intrigue, it wasn't clear exactly whom Justin had left the awards ceremony with. The previous night's events were pored over in minute detail, like a Watergate exposé for the tabloid generation. It was no secret that Dannii, Kylie and Justin enjoyed dinner with their assistants and minders at the Montpeliano Restaurant.

The melting pot of rumour was fuelled by the fact that Kylie was still embroiled in a very public split from her former lover, James Gooding. Kylie had arrived at EMI's post-Brits party with Dannii, Janet Jackson and Justin. There were reports that Gooding rowed with Kylie at this party but stories of him standing outside Kylie's flat while she was in fact with Justin were flatly denied by James. He often found himself unfairly cast as the bad boy in the whole saga as the media were desperate to perpetuate any supposed Kylie–Justin affair. However, at first it appeared that after this supposed confrontation with Gooding, Kylie seemingly went to her hotel to retire.

However, all was not as it seemed. At first, the press announced that Justin had spent the night with Kylie's prettier but less popular sister, Dannii. Photos splashed across the front pages showed the pair pulling up outside the posh Mandarin Oriental Hotel in swish Knightsbridge at 3.40 a.m. The theory ran that the paparazzi took their shots and retired home for the (late) night. It later transpired that the clever money was actually on Kylie being Justin's paramour for the evening after all.

Unbeknown to all but the sharpest of showbiz reporters – most notably that oracle of pop, Rav Singh of the *News of the World* – this apparent tryst with Dannii had all been a decoy. Only fifteen minutes after Justin had entered the Mandarin, Kylie had slipped into the same hotel. Both stars also invited their entourages to the same private party in Justin's suite, however. Nonetheless, Kylie was spotted leaving by a back entrance at 6 a.m. Justin checked out of the same hotel at 9 a.m.

Quite what Dannii made of all this was uncertain, particularly as her own pop career had been beleaguered with constant comparisons to her more successful sister. She did, however, admit to not entering the Mandarin at all, instead heading home to her luxury apartment in Battersea. The showbiz gossip circuit – which celebs often deliberately fuel as much as try to avoid – had been reinforcing the Justin–Dannii line to distract from Kylie's involvement.

While James Gooding openly despaired of the 'negative press' he was tired of getting, Justin and Kylie seemed to bask in the spotlight. The weekend after the Brits she flew to New York where she jointly presented a Grammy with Justin (arriving in a blacked out car with registration plate DIVA 1). Here they shamelessly flirted on stage some more – Justin even suggestively quipped, 'Can I grab your ass again?' Notably, Kylie was for once wearing a fashion disaster, which looked like a peculiar mutation of a shower splashback

inbred with tissue paper, while a far more stylish Justin wore a black suit, black tie and black shirt. Kylie had been nominated in the 'Best Dance Recording' award for her single 'Love At First Sight'. They went to separate post-Grammy parties but met up later in the night at a special birthday party thrown for Drew Barrymore by her co-stars in the Charlie's Angels films, Cameron Diaz and Lucy Liu. However, the star duo stayed that night in hotels at almost opposite ends of Manhattan.

Yet, despite all this high profile 'canoodling', Kylie and Justin are not an item. No one seemed to mention the twelve-year age gap, but then Kylie is perceived as a Peter Pan of female pop. Hardly Sir Cliff, but when you consider she had her first UK chart hit when Justin was only seven years old, it seemed that the life of a pop diva

had been kind to Ms Minogue in more ways than one. And just to add a final twist, by late March 2003, reports suggested that James Gooding and Kylie might be an item once again. Kylie's spokesman said they were 'still friends', while James told the media they still loved each other. Justin, notably, kept silent.

Realistically speaking, the enormous success of Justin's solo album *Justified* does not bode well for any future 'N Sync album. After all, is it really feasible, with Justin's personal currency running so high, for him to go back out on tour and in the studio as just one cog in a five-piece group? Industry rumours suggest that some members of 'N Sync are unhappy with the generous support given to JT by Jive Records. JC was also trying to establish a solo career of his own and to

'WE'RE YOUNG GUYS, WE LIKE TO HAVE FUN, AND WE MAKE MISTAKES SOMETIMES'

many observers it seemed as though he was not getting the same level of backing. Maybe that aforementioned 'N Sync show in Orlando in April 2003 will be the band's last after all. To his credit, Justin is at pains to play down such whispers. 'We're scheduled to go back in the studio [late 2003] sometime, to make another record,' he insists. 'So rest assured, I seriously mean it when I say with all the confidence in the world [that] I think we'll make another record.'

So where next for Justin Timberlake? Having previously played a minor role in the TV movie *Model Behaviour* alongside Maggie Lawson and Kathie Lee Gifford, maybe a career in the movies beckons. Rumours abound of other potential film offers flooding in, including *Grease 3* and Fox Television's supposed hip-hop adaptation of The *Wizard Of Oz*. However, in light of the huge success of his solo project, it seems unlikely he will have the time for such career moves.

Musically, he has the world at his feet. Since the critical acclaim and commercial success achieved by *Justified*, he has been approached by legions of the world's top producers, writers, studio wizards and fellow pop stars. Wherever his muse takes him next, he is sure to be accompanied by some of the world's biggest names.

Romantically, he might be back with Britney or off to a club with another in a long line of famous beauties. He has so many difficult choices to make.

Suffice it to say, by the tender age of 22, Justin Timberlake has already achieved far more than most artists could ever dream of in an entire career. Where he goes to next is anybody's guess, but one thing is certain: it will be one hell of a ride finding out.